Wings to Victory

LAURIE MARKS VINCENT

LAURIE MARKS VINCENT

Copyright © 2014 – 2017 – 2022 Laurie Marks Vincent

Third Edition

All rights reserved.

ISBN:
ISBN-13:
978-1537421223

ISBN-10:
1537421220

DEDICATION

To my husband Scott and our two boys, Brandon and Kyle, who were caught with me in the storm. After God, Scott you were constant. Your faith in God made it possible for me to press forward. I'm so glad that we've had these years together and look forward to the many more to come. For all of my family and especially my children, their spouses, and grandchildren, I hope you'll see the miracle you are to me and God. I pray that you will understand the mysteries of God, his saving grace, and the blessings that he has for you when you simply believe his Words.

CONTENTS

1	We Are Family	Pg 10
2	The God Shift	Pg 16
3	Love Like a Flood	Pg 26
4	The Witnesses	Pg 33
5	A Word in the Rainbow	Pg 46
6	The Journey Begins	Pg 56
7	Awakened	Pg 68
8	Lions & Trumpets	Pg 81
9	A Change of Space	Pg 95
10	A Song in the Night	Pg 109
11	Behold Snakes & Angels	Pg 122
12	The Snake Exposed	Pg 133
13	New Wings	Pg 140
14	Mysteries Revealed	Pg 149
15	The Whole Woman	Pg 164

WINGS TO VICTORY

ACKNOWLEDGMENTS

Special thanks to my friend, Linda, who was my second set of eyes in the writing process of this story.

Thank you for my "lady friends" (you know who you are) on social networks that encouraged me to share the whole story.

Artwork *- Cover design and drawings in chapter 7 by Laurie Marks Vincent*

WINGS TO VICTORY

Introduction

Although I had received healing supernaturally, it seemed magical in the past. It was amazing. I was always grateful and in awe, yet the mystery remained. I knew the source of the miracle and the source of the power, but what was it in me that caused my faith to receive this miracle? I was haunted by scripture that seemed as though it was written like a riddle.

"Now faith is the substance of things hoped for, the evidence of things not seen." -- Hebrews 11:1 (KJV)

I went over the words repeatedly, dissected them, and broke them down, over and over in my head. I played them out in my life as I tried to comprehend the spiritual application. Did I make it too complicated? I have highlighted the prominent and most important memories of this story. Those 13 years may have seemed like a lifetime, but the things that I learned during this self-discovery journey with God are only a mere whisper of my lifetime.

WINGS TO VICTORY

1 We Are Family

As a child, family life was great, loving and caring parents, sibling rivalry, lots of music, family camping trips, and great Christmas family gatherings. It's all a part of our house's healthy and balanced family dynamics. Well, at least this was my normal, but maybe not so balanced all the time. Looking back, it was never a fairy tale childhood, but I know my parents did their best.

I am the oldest of four children. I have a younger sister and two younger brothers. We were all encouraged to pursue our gifts, talents, and dreams, which is one of the reasons why I usually walk in confidence today, especially when I focus on the Lord. I have always believed He is with me. I had to be infused with that confidence because life had some physical limitations for me at a very young age. I only grew to 4 feet and 11 inches tall. Over the years, I have shrunk too, but it was no surprise to my family. There were generations before me, including my mother, who were just the same. My height is still my biggest roadblock with physical limitations for me.

Even as I write this, I think I might be shrinking. I remember my mother telling me what the doctor said when I was born. After he finished examining me he said, "Well, she's just a little thing but she's all there! Ten fingers and ten toes!"

My fondest memories with my Grandparents. They were very influential to my faith. I would stay for a week or two with my Grandma and Grandpa Fair during the summer holidays. Every night before bed, the three of us would gather around the kitchen table. Grandpa would read a whole chapter of the Bible and then we would pray for each family member in need. This was an extremely powerful time. We would lift our heads from praying to wipe away tears from our faces. You could not ignore the fact that the presence of God had visited us at that moment.

I would also spend a week or two at a Christian Camp with my other Grandparents, Grandma and Grandpa Garon. The camp today is called Braeside Bible Conference Grounds. I attended Children's Church in the little chapel that was just down the road from our cabin. The Children's service would always finish early.

While other children would go to the park to play and wait for the Adult service to finish, I was still hungry for God. I would go to the Adult Service and scan the top of people's heads until I spotted my grandparents. It was easy to identify the big wave of hair on the top of my Grandpa's head. I would spend the remainder of the evening in the Adult Service, waiting to see what God would do after the preacher finished his message and the altar service had started.

It was during one of those Summer camp days at Children's Church that I accepted Jesus as my personal Saviour. I thought that I was should experience a lightning bolt of power, so I kept asking him into my heart. Perhaps my request had been intercepted. Hey! I was just a little kid. No one told me that I only had to ask "by faith" once. After about 11 times, I figured it out. He is a gentle pursuer of my love and life.

It was a regular part of family life, to attend church every Sunday and be involved in church activities. You would find me and my sister, along with my brothers, occasionally singing a special song during the church service. Our church services aired on the local radio station on Sunday mornings and so listeners would hear us "live" on the radio. We were also involved in Talent Searches too. Together, my sister and I had won several vocal competitions. I remember when my Uncle Al once brought us a dozen red roses when we returned home from a competition. Uncle Gillis would sit and draw cartoons with me and my Aunt Rose always would sing with me, "I beg your pardon, I never promised you a rose garden". When I was very young, I called her "Auntie Bow" because she wore bows in her hair. It also wasn't unusual to be in the passenger seat of the car with one of my many Aunts, my Mother's sisters, and we'd be singing to a song on the radio or a Gospel cassette. All of our Aunts and Uncles had talents, love, and friendship that they shared with us.

There have been times in my life, because of my size, I felt people didn't hear me. Perhaps they regarded me as insignificant. I do know the difference between when someone ignores me, avoids me, and when they respond. However, insecurities can play a strong role in our identity, so I found my confidence in what I could do well. I did it well with a sincere heart to please the Lord, and I never settled for "good enough". I pursued it with good intentions and with excellence. Mostly, I drew this from my love for singing and I learned right beside the best of them. Sandi Patty, Amy Grant, and Evie were my girlfriends. I was mentored through almost every single album they ever released. Sandi may have been singing on that record but the Holy Spirit was the one who was teaching me.

The very first concerts I ever attended were a Sandi Patty and Evie concert. I asked and my parents were glad to buy tickets so that we could all go. It was awesome!

And now ….

This is where things become complex. While the present is running on a timeline, we don't realize that our present timeline, our day-to-day life, is affected by our past. This is because our past haunts us until our dying day unless we tend to it in the present. Skeletons in the closet will rear their ugly heads, and we quickly attempt to shut the door and hope they never expose us. Generation after generation can break down a family. Alcoholism and pain from the past, if not dealt with, can drive a person to their destruction unless the Lord steps in to save them. At the time I am writing this, I'm so happy to say that although the enemy came to kill, steal and destroy, God has stepped in and His amazing grace has brought redemption. The story is one of the past, but all of it leads to revealing God's goodness and faithfulness.

WINGS TO VICTORY

2 The God Shift

After high school, I had a part-time job downtown. Walking home from work one day I met a young man that was passing through town. He was a traveling salesman. He stopped to ask for directions. Our meeting caused him to stay in town. He proposed after a few months and we were engaged by Christmas that same year.

One afternoon, he drove into the driveway. My dad met him in the driveway. Watching from the side door, I don't know what the conversation was about, but I believe my dad was testing him. I also think that my dad saw something in this young man that reminded my dad of himself. Suddenly, I saw my dad punch him in the stomach. My fiancé's face showed pain as he held his stomach. He never retaliated by throwing another punch. He knew it would not turn out well if he tried to fight back. My dad was much larger and taller. Later, my fiancé said he could press charges but he wasn't going to ask me to witness against my father. I do believe my dad apologized later but that was the most conversation or interaction they would ever have from that time forward.

Attending church every Sunday with me, he was trying to live for the Lord but his old and worldly ways were detrimental to our relationship. He cheated on me with one of my friends. I forgave him. He confessed it to me with all sincerity, because he knew he had to make it right. I think forgiving him was easier because he confessed and after all, love forgives. Within a day afterward, my friend came to me and told me what he had done. I told her he had confessed and I forgave him. Going forward with the relationship was now about seeing what change God would do in him. I knew that trust was broken though and I would have to keep that in check to see if our relationship would heal.

He fed me dreams that would never become a reality. My heart was always about serving the Lord in ministry, at some level. He promised me all the things a girl would want to hear about "being in ministry together". Although I believe he wanted to and his intentions were good, he would never be able to follow through. He did take me on a few ministry engagements where I was singing at different churches and a local television appearance. However, the enemy had created such deception and our relationship was so divisive that I ran away from home.

I found refuge at a boarding house in town. The lady who owned the boarding house was a Christian. She was wise with a gentle spirit, in her senior years. We had many great conversations. Since I was a border, she didn't have to, but she cooked dinner and we ate together. I knew God had placed her in my life for a purpose. I look back now and realized how God was using her. She was praying for me. She never interfered. She just loved me. My fiancé would visit in the evening but because of hurtles in the past with him, my guard was up.

On one particular evening, our visit ended, we stood on the front porch and talked for a few minutes. He kissed me goodnight and said he was going straight home to bed.

Yet, when I watched him get into his truck, I heard a voice say, "No he's not going home. Watch his truck. He's going to the bar."

My eyes followed the tail lights of his truck as it headed in the direction of the Royal Tavern. Immediately, I headed in that direction. I had a raging determination in my step as I walk over to the bar, and caught him in "the act". To say the least, I was just waiting for another reason to break off the relationship. God led me right to it. It was never talked about, nor was it "public knowledge" but I grew up with a father who was a closet alcoholic, trying to secretly drown his pain. As a result, I was uncomfortable around alcohol. I had seen the brokenness, dysfunction, and deception through over-indulgence. I chose not to take a chance that I may have to live with. I was done waiting for change, knowing that change would never happen after we were married. I knew I would be settling for something that was not God's will. Most definitely, the voice I heard warning me that night was the voice of the Holy Spirit.

My dad said to my mom, "This was not good, but I know Laurie would have made it work because that's the kind of person she is."

I took over his apartment for a while, but it was not a place I wanted to stay. Eventually, I returned home.

I took the furniture from his apartment and sold it all in a lawn sale to recoup my losses. He later returned and begged to reconcile. My parents were compassionate. He had a broken heart and they comforted him but told him this marriage was not going to happen. I remember when my mom held him as he cried. He was in a place of desperation. In the days ahead, he kept trying to sway me and so my parents sent me to Braeside Camp for a Christian Singles Retreat. If I recall correctly, it was my friend Marilyn who had suggested the retreat. You'll hear more about Marilyn later in the story.

I called my Grandma and asked to stay at her cabin so that I could attend the retreat.

She agreed and said, "of course."

Grandma had this cabin when I was a young girl. I remember staying at camp for a week with her, in this very cabin. She reminded me of how the stove works and the locks on the windows and doors. Since another cabin had been connected with an adjoining wall to the original cabin, there was now a separate bedroom and little half bath. Oh good! I would not have to walk to the camp washroom around the corner or pee in a pail at night!

The retreat was amazing but I kept mostly to myself. I didn't make any friends. I just attended the amazing worship services and returned to the cabin, spending time alone, just me and God.

After one of the evening worship services, the message was done and I responded to the altar call. I needed Jesus to heal my heart. In shame, I went to the altar and knelt behind the piano. I thought I was well hidden, but three ladies stormed into my space. Two stood behind me and one kneeling in front of me. I was a mess as they prayed passionately like they were on fire. Suddenly I heard the woman in front of me begin to speak in a very comforting voice, telling me things that God wanted me to know. She told me so many wonderful things about how I am a treasured daughter and He rejoices over me. There isn't much else that I remember except this next thing. She said, "Your husband is just around the corner, and together you will have a ministry with limitless borders."

The words, "limitless borders" still confound me to this day but in this digital age, I can see how this would be possible today.

I returned home and the whirlwind had stopped. My ex-fiancé had found a way to get a plane ticket home. I felt new and could see clearly again.

I was praying about where I should go, and what I should do as I continued this season of healing. I had already surrendered the prophetic words spoken over me that night at the altar. Things were still fresh for me. I felt I had to pick myself up and get some direction. What or where is that next step? That evening, my father heard me crying in my room. He slowly opened my door and asked why I was crying. I told him, "I didn't know what God wanted me to do now." Gently he said, "I don't know the answer, but I know he will show you." Then, he closed the door.

Shortly afterward, a friend of mine suggested that I visit Toronto to see what ministry opportunities might be available. He arranged for me to stay with his friend Kim. Her sister would be away that weekend and so there would be room for me to stay with her. During one of my weekend visits to Toronto, Kim's sister came home and decided to move out. Kim needed a roommate and so I stayed. In January 1987, I applied for social services to help with finances and my mom shipped more of my things on the bus for me to pick up later. I spent my mornings with God, reading the Word and journaling. I was on my own now, looking to God to direct my next steps. One early morning while I was spending time with the Lord, I opened my Bible. It was then that I wrote my first song entitled, "Trust in Me". I was amazed at the way God had flooded this song from my soul as I read his Word.

"Trust in the Lord with all your heart and do not lean on your own understanding. 6 In all your ways acknowledge Him, and He will make your paths straight."

-- Proverbs 3:5,6

Kim worked at 100 Huntley Street. She worked in the department where they receive phone calls from those who called the ministry for prayer. In our conversation one day we took some time to pray about specific needs.

After we finished praying, she looked at me and said, "God wants you to apply for a job at 100 Huntley Street." This was the first Canadian Christian television show on a major television network. It was under the umbrella of Crossroads Christian Communications started by Pastor David Mainse and his wife, Norma Jean.

In February 1987 I was assigned a position in the same department as Kim. My job was to pray for others. How awesome is that? There were a number of us who worked together on the phones in the same room at every shift, 24 hours a day. We saw many miracles and answered prayers each day.

I remember praying with a Mother who called for her young daughter. The little girl had pink eye. She sat her little girl on her knee and listened on the phone as I began to pray. Only a few sentences into my prayer and I hear the mother gasp. I stop praying and ask her, "What's wrong?"

The overwhelming joy in her voice was a surprise when I heard her say, "I just watched all the redness and infection leave her eye. Her eye is completely healed."

You can imagine the shouts of joy in the prayer department that day!

The night shift came with a whole new set of circumstances. There was no shortage of lonely people who needed to talk in the middle of the night. We were also not counselors and so we only offered to pray for them. As well, some pranksters called to throw you off. Some who played like demons and some who perhaps could very well have been possessed. When those phone calls happened, one of my new friends named "Sanj" would just remind me that the devil likes to see you jump, so don't let it get at you.

There was good fellowship among the prayer team members. When we worked the night shift, we would stop for breakfast at a restaurant just around the corner before we all jumped on the subway and went our separate ways for some well-deserved sleep.

Sometimes it was hard not to take the burdens of others home with you. The prayer requests came in varying degrees of trials, needs, and burdens. It was always good to take time after a shift and ask the Lord to lift the burdens and heaviness away. One night, I came home from a very troublesome night shift and asked the Holy Spirit to minister to me. As I drifted to sleep, I heard a beautiful voice singing words of comfort and love to me. It was breathtaking and I had never heard something that touched me so deeply. Startled by hearing the voice, I stirred from nearly falling asleep and opened my eyes to look around. Kim was not home. It could have only been an angel or the voice of the Spirit of God singing over me.

"For the LORD your God is living among you. He is a mighty savior. He will take delight in you with gladness. With his love, he will calm all your fears. He will rejoice over you with joyful songs."

– Zephaniah 3:17

WINGS TO VICTORY

3 Love like a Flood

One night before a shift, I went to a room reserved for staff who wanted to pray alone. Valentine's Day had passed and it had seemed a little, well to be honest... lonely and disappointing. That night, I surrendered all those feelings in exchange for peace and surety that God would keep my heart single-minded toward him. I turned off the radar and didn't think twice or turn my head once to wonder, "Was he the one?"

The night shift was sometimes very troubling and heavy because this is when people often see the darkest times in their life. It was only a few hours since I had started a shift and a phone call came in on my line for prayer. This call was different than the rest. I heard the voice of an older gentleman who had a kind and soft voice. He also had a Southern accent. This is not something that you would hear often since 100 Huntley Street is widely known as a Canadian program. It made me very curious since he said he was from Georgia! He began to share that the Holy Spirit had moved him to call this number because God was calling him to pray for someone on the other end of the line. Now, this was a switch! Instead of praying for others on that night, God had moved someone to call and pray for me. He didn't ask if I had a prayer request or a special need. He just started praying. A few minutes into prayer, God was revealing a vision to him. Describing what God was showing him, he told me that my husband would have a red tint in his hair and beard when the sun hit it. He said that he could see us holding two children. He knew the first was a boy but God didn't reveal if the second child was a boy or girl. His voice exuded joy as he said that my husband stood looking over me, we would have a ministry together, and that I will know him when he says, "He just came off the mission field."

I so wish that this call had been recorded for "training purposes" because I would have loved to have a copy of this call. I know that he said so much more, but my memory has never been able to recall it. I have remembered the points that struck me the most when I first heard them. This was a moment I kept to myself and never told my roommate Kim.

A week later, I'm working the day shift and I have to leave my post to go to Val Dodd's office. I needed some information for a caller and I knew Val would have it. I passed a young man who looked like he was wandering the hall, so I asked if he needed any help.

"I'm just looking for a public telephone that I can use. "

I directed him to the phone at the front desk and returned to my desk in the prayer room.

Prayer Team members were always placed in the studio and captured occasionally on camera during the program. My Grandma Garon would tell me she would watch the show and look for me when the camera caught the prayer team in the studio. There was also a live studio audience each day. The next day, the young man was back again. I felt as though someone was watching me while I was on the phone during the program in the studio. I looked over to the studio audience and there he was. After the program was over, he was one of the last to walk across the studio floor. Audience members were able to go to lunch in the cafeteria where everyone from staff, program hosts, and audience members could mingle together. I knew he was alone and so I asked him if he would like to join me at my table for lunch.

He said, "Sure," and introduced himself to me, "Hi, my name is Scott by the way."

I smiled and told him my name as we headed to the cafeteria. We picked up our food in line and sat down at the table. Something about him felt strangely familiar yet I had never met him before the other day. I asked him where he was from.

"I'm from Midland Ontario, a small town up north of Toronto. I'm visiting a friend for the week."

"That's nice!" I said, "and so what do you do?"

His eyes lit up as he said to me, "I just came off the mission field."

At that very second, the Prayer Team Supervisor, Geri, called all the prayer team members into the prayer room. It was like flash lightening in my head, recalling the words of the caller that late night who had a vision of my husband. I never had a chance to even show a reaction as the words, "I just came off the mission field" rang in my head. Geri was calling the prayer team from their lunch hour because all the phones were ringing off the hook in the prayer room. This has never happened before and we were never allowed to bring our lunch into the prayer room. An exception was made that day. I apologized to Scott as I had to remove myself from the table with my lunch.

Later that afternoon, I went on my break and found him still sitting in the cafeteria.

"Hey! You're still here. I'm sorry about having to leave. The phones have never been so busy right after a program."

There was a little smile in his eyes, "That's okay. Ya, I'm hoping I can get some direction. I'd like to find a church that has a mid-week service for College and Career Groups."

I asked him if he would wait one moment. He agreed, and then I directed him to Val Dodd's office.

Later I saw him in the halls again. "Did you find the information that you were looking for?"

"Yes, thank you very much. I just finished seeing Mr. Dodd. He told me about a College and Career Night at Queensway Cathedral that's happening on Wednesday. I just need to find a ride."

My eyes smiled as I responded to him.

"Oh, that's the same College and Career that I go to. Unfortunately, I bus it everywhere in the city and so I can't provide a ride," I told him.

"That's okay. Something will work out," he responded.

"Well, I hope to see you there," I told him.

I returned to my desk in the prayer room to complete my shift. Little did I know that someone did offer him a ride to the church that night for College and a Career.

When I arrived at the church, I immediately spotted Scott. I have no idea how he was able to arrange a ride, but he came in with a young lady. She just happened to be his ride to church that evening. I greeted them both and asked if they had seats yet. I offered them both a seat where I was sitting. He sat beside me and the young lady who gave Scott a ride sat on his other side. Scott didn't bring a Bible with him and so I shared my Bible with him. She also shared her Bible with him and so began the question of who's Bible he would share. My Bible landed on his lap first and so he turned to me and looked over at my Bible. After the service was over, we all went out for coffee. The young lady who gave him a ride had a van and so we all went together with her. Scott and I had a great conversation and the young lady who gave him a ride seemed to sit back and watch, although she engaged in conversation a little here and there with everyone. Scott shared with me that he was staying with a friend for the week and just checking out the sights in Toronto. This is the main reason why he had visited 100 Huntley Street Studios. Our conversation quickly developed into common interests and friendship. I told him that tomorrow was my day off and so we decided to meet at my place for pizza the next day.

Kim was working that following day. A knock came on the door and I met Scott at my apartment door. He came in and I ordered pizza. We sat and talked and enjoyed pizza and learned more about each other. Our conversation ended with the supernatural realization that God had set up our meeting.

It was weeks later that Scott and I tried to find the

young woman who gave Scott a ride to College and Career at Queensway that night. She never was at a prior meeting that I attended and we never saw her at a meeting again. We started putting the pieces of the puzzle together when Scott told me that she showed up at 100 Huntley Street, shortly after Val Dodd gave him the information about that first College and Career Night at Queensway Church. It was a divine setup.

4 The Witnesses

It was a quiet afternoon. Kim and I both had the day off. I had not mentioned a single thing to Kim about Scott. She did not know that Scott existed. We were both in our bedrooms, relaxing and reading our Bibles. The peace of God was so evident at that time. Suddenly, Kim jetted from her bedroom with overwhelming wonder.

"Laurie, I was just reading this scripture and I just know it's for you."

I sat up and asked her, "What is it?"

"Here! I'll read it to you."

She sat down on the side of my bed and held her Bible up as she focused on Isaiah Chapter 62.

"Because I love Zion, I will not keep still. Because my heart yearns for Jerusalem, I cannot remain silent. I will not stop praying for her until her righteousness shines like the dawn and her salvation blazes like a burning torch. ² The nations will see your righteousness. World leaders will be blinded by your glory. And you will be given a new name by the Lord's own mouth. ³ The Lord will hold you in his hand for all to see— a splendid crown in the hand of God. ⁴ Never again will you be called "The Forsaken City" or "The Desolate Land." Your new name will be "The City of God's Delight" and "The Bride of God," for the Lord delights in you and will claim you as his bride. ⁵ Your children will commit themselves to you, O Jerusalem, just as a young man commits himself to his bride. Then God will rejoice over you as a bridegroom rejoices over his bride." – Isaiah 62:1-5 NLT

As she read it, I knew that the bigger picture of this scripture was for Israel, but there were "code words" God was causing to jump out to me, that he knew I would associate with, not to mention the whole scripture was about a bride and his bridegroom. That was the big "give away". Up to this point, I had been asking God for confirmation about Scott. I had received that ominous word from a stranger over the phone on the night shift a few weeks ago, but I wanted something more to ensure this was truly God. Words in this scripture such as "new name", and "splendid crown" as well as "bride", were clear indications that God was confirming his plan for Scott and me.

I sat there and listened to Kim read the scripture while I kept a straight face. I asked her to read it again because my spirit witnessed what God was saying specifically to me. My heart was reveling in what I already knew.

I still kept it in my heart as Kim looked at me, "There ya go. God says that scripture is for you."

I thanked her and she turned around and went back into her bedroom smiling from ear to ear.

Scott had gone home to Midland and promised to return with plans to stay in Toronto. He also had some profound experiences that affirmed God's plan for marriage.

His Pastor had asked that Scott accompany him to visit a troubled young man. Pastor Ron had set up this appointment but brought Scott along for surety. Scott had experience in Martial Arts and thought that Scott was good protection and that there was purpose in meeting this young man. Together, in the Pastor's car, Scott and Pastor Ron sat in the driveway but discovered there was no one home. On the drive back, Scott and Pastor Ron had a chance to talk.

"You met someone when you were in Toronto, didn't you?

Scott must have wondered how much was showing on his face, but asked him, "How did you know?"

"God showed me a vision of her. She is not very tall, she has soft brown hair, shoulder-length, and a big smile."

Scott reached into his Bible, a little shocked, and pulled out a picture of me, that I had given him."

"Yep, that's her." Pastor Ron grinned. "That's the woman God showed me."

While Scott was home, he met up with his buddy Tony. Tony offered to take Scott back to the bus stop when he returned to Toronto. The day came, and Tony picked up Scott and took him to the bus stop. Tony walked Scott over to the bus stop and they talked for a little while. Scott never mentioned me. He was just hoping the bus would come quickly. He wanted to get back to Toronto. The bus pulled up and Scott picked up his luggage.

Tony stopped Scott to get his attention. "By the way Scott, God showed me that the woman you met in Toronto is the woman he wants you to marry."

As he got on the bus, his face looked shocked then he smiled, with a little chuckle. "Thanks, man! See ya later".

When Scott returned, we exchanged stories and laughed with excitement at what God was doing. It was no doubt. We liked each other, however, we did not discover a love for one another until after. God was match-making before we even discovered we loved each other. It wasn't love at first sight. It was, "God? Is this the one you have chosen for me?"

In March, Scott joined the Huntley Street family as a security guard and also worked part-time on the prayer team phones. Scott found a very small apartment in an area of Toronto called, "Painted Post". I only visited his apartment twice. I was feeling very uneasy about the fact that it was a shared space with a dim and grungy print shop. Very unusual, but it contained a bed, a small refrigerator, stovetop, and bathroom. It was only a pit stop.

Our relationship grew and we found ourselves committed to one another. Although, we had one good fight and there was a moment of uncertainty in our relationship. It quickly dissipated over 24 hours while we were working at 100 Huntley Street. The one thing that was clear about 100 Huntley Street is that there were a few other couples at Huntley who were also engaged as well. It was quite the "love boat" at that time. We both continued working there until about July that year, 1987. I was wearing thin with shift changes. They were becoming too short to adapt from day shift to night shift and back again. It was affecting my sleep cycles terribly. I was not feeling like myself emotionally and felt so drained spiritually. I went on to find a new job, with a cleaning service in the city. It was just before then that Scott and I were officially engaged in May 1987, of the very same year we met.

I moved from the apartment that I shared with Kim shortly after we both left Huntley Street. I found a boarding house run by a Christian lady in Guildwood Parkway. The boys were downstairs and the girls were upstairs. When a room opened up for Scott, he did not hesitate to move out of the dim little space at "Painted Post". We lived under the same roof and shared meals every day. He landed an awesome job with a tour company, as a driver. He made daily trips to the Niagara sites with tourists each day. His tips were as good as his paycheck and he always came home with fresh fruit from the Niagara Escarpment fruit stands. Each time that he stopped there with the tourists, the fruit stand owners gave him free fruit, because he brought in the tourists that gave them business.

These were days for God's favor and miracles. Often there were times when many of us in the boarding house would do a potluck dinner and share a meal. At one particular meal, each of us was just putting together what we had left until "payday". Gloria, our housemother had seven potatoes left. She prepared them, cutting each potato in half, and cooked them up. Fourteen pieces of potato were placed in a bowl with the rest of the food on the table. Seven of us sat at the table to eat. We said grace and enjoyed our meal and had some great laughs and fellowship together. As we were cleaning up, Gloria noticed that there were still potatoes left in the bowl. We all attested to having at least two pieces of potato among seven of us. It was astounding to realize that there were still potatoes left. I remember the look of joy and surprise on Gloria's face. We were all amazed and just thanked the Lord again. That day God multiplied the potatoes!

We didn't have a lot of money. When Scott decided to leave 100 Huntley Street he took his last paycheck from 100 Huntley and bought my engagement ring and all of our wedding rings. We didn't even plan to buy wedding rings. We just walked into Ostrander Jewelers at Yorkdale Mall, window shopping. We saw the sale sign and picked them out on spur of the moment.

No one knew, but on a visit home to see my parents, Scott came with me. My mom joined Scott and me at a coffee shop in the mall. We never mentioned anything about rings. After some conversation, she looks at us with a grin on her face.

"Just give me six months!"

I thought to myself, "How did she know? Was it that obvious?"

Our courtship was a whirlwind of divine appointments. Again, not a lot of money. No special flower arrangements on the church platform. The Bride and Groom were the main attraction. We bought a small flower wedding package that included the essentials. Corsages, boutonnieres and my bouquet. My mom made the girl's dresses for the wedding party. On another visit home, my mom and I went to a fabric store and picked out a pattern for a wedding dress. I chose a satin material that was layered under a French embossed lace. It had roses embossed along the scalloped edge of the material. The sales lady at the store said they had never had anything in the store like it before. It was truly beautiful with a slight shimmer to the thread that made the roses. The roses were significant because, during a visit to Midland to meet Scott's mom, he showed me a poem he wrote in high school. He won an award at school for this poem. The day he showed it to me, he handed the paper to me to keep.

We were married on November seventh, the same year that we met, 1987. The family brought desserts, just like at our family Christmas gatherings. My Aunt Ruth made cake wrapped in little paper doilies for wedding guest favors. My cousin Kevin picked out the design for the wedding cake. My dad and Scott's brother Stuart did the wedding photography. These are things I hadn't even thought about, but my family was busy working on them. I just had stars in my eyes and these details never crossed my mind. The one thing we did look after was the meal at the reception. The chef from the cafeteria at 100 Huntley Street made our buffet-style meal. It was such a blessing.

We still laugh today about how Scott decided that he had to go to the bathroom just before the ceremony started. Pastor Ron, who married us, told him it was too late and he didn't get to go the bathroom until it was time to take wedding party photos after the ceremony.

There was one unusual thing that stood out. It happened after the ceremony in the receiving line. There was an elderly couple who stood in line. They stepped up to us when their time came, and reached their hands out to us to shake our hands. They looked adorable together with kind faces and bright eyes.

Smiling with delight, she speaks up, "We've been waiting for this day a long time."

We smiled and said, "thank you".

They continued to move through the receiving line and then Scott and I looked at each other.

"I've never seen them before. Do you know who they are?" I asked Scott.

"No, I have no idea." He shrugged his shoulders. To this day, we have always wondered who these special visitors were and why they had been waiting for this day for a "long time." Did witnesses visit from heaven? Were we entertaining angels unaware?

After we were married, I was now working for a cleaning company. I had injured myself at work and was now suffering from an injury to my lower back, neck, and shoulders. The injury took place just two months after we were married, I also discovered that I was pregnant with our first child. We did not want to start a family in Toronto and so we moved back to my hometown of Tillsonburg and stayed with my parents for a few months. I was rapidly expanding as the baby grew and my whole pregnancy was a challenge, right from the beginning. I was still recovering from the injury to my neck, shoulders, and lower back, and then I was pregnant too! I never felt well, constantly sore, in pain, and sick. My favorite craving and diversion from the wrong food was an apple.

We were staying at my parent's home while we re-situated ourselves. My goodness! I was still writing out thank-you notes for wedding gifts at that time too. We had a plan and of course, things had to come into order. Scott needed a job and we needed to find a home of our own before the baby arrived.

While we were staying with my parents, there was one little scare while I was pregnant. I lost my balance and fell down a flight of stairs. If the stairs were a slide it would have been much more fun. I ended up with a very bruised tailbone that I would endure for more than a year, but the baby was absolutely fine.

In the middle of one night, my younger brother came into our bedroom and shook my shoulder to wake me. I remember seeing his broad shoulders outlined in a silhouette as the light from the moon shone through the bedroom window behind him.

"Laurie, Laurie, wake up!", he said with a loud and

urgent whisper.

Startled, I opened my eyes, "What?"

All through my childhood, there had been more than one altercation between my parents and so their marriage had a lot of trouble. Yes, parents fight, but these episodes were "over the top."

Except for the heaviness I felt in my body as I lay there, I don't remember anything after that moment. I simply don't remember what happened after that. In the days ahead, I returned to the familiar need to walk on eggshells just as when I was a child. I walked on eggshells but pretended that nothing was wrong. It was for fear of another outburst. This was not the first time, and this would not be the last, but I had to let each incident go by as though it had not happened. It's important to know that this shaped fears, my own personal behavioral traits, perceptions, and views, as well as attitudes. It must have been the same for my dad and his childhood. His skeleton in the closet reared its ugly head and I began to see and understand a generational cycle of wounded childhood, emptiness, alcoholism, and abuse. In general, the smallest little thing was magnified by generations of anger and tempers flaring from unresolved wounds in the soul. The simple need to be valued can become the focus and be overemphasized because the scale of that need is large. As an adult, co-dependency is apparent because of habitual "closet" addictions. There is no control over them and that is why they are addictions. This became clearer as I observed the generational pain. Perhaps by remaining in secret, the purpose was to prevent conflict and disappointment with others.

WINGS TO VICTORY

5

A Word in the Rainbow

My dad was a supervisor at a car factory and had put a good word in for Scott. In a few weeks, Scott got the job, and we started to shop for furniture and other things that we would need for our own home. A friend from the church had kept her ears and eyes open for us and found a little white two-bedroom house at the top of the hill, at the end of town. I told her no orange shag carpet. She promised. Instead, it was an orange loop carpet. Can you see my eyes rolling as I think about the moment I saw the carpet? The little house was just down the road from my mom and dad. It was very old and in need of some serious repair. I remember, in my frail condition, frantically crying as I told my mom that the kitchen was terrible because the cupboard doors had been papered with shiny mac-tac paper in awful 60s patterns of orange and blue flowers.

In the days that followed, while Scott was at work, my mom and I went over to the house. I would keep her company while she peeled several layers of old mac-tac paper from the front of the kitchen cupboard doors. The same designer touch had been used to "renew" their look over the years. We cleaned them and painted them in a simple clean white.

We paid $200.00 for rent each month. This was unheard of but in exchange for the low rent, our only requirement was to take care of the many gardens planted by the current owner, a retired lady who had gone into the nursing home. Despite some repairs and a necessary makeover, we moved in and I decorated the home with a light airy feeling. The dining room window opened like old balcony doors but had glass shelves in front where I placed items that sparkled when the light hit them. White sheers framed all the windows in the house except for the kitchen, where I accented with the color red. There were so many other good reasons why we couldn't turn away from its nostalgic and cottage-style charm.

On October 17th, the day was as usual. Scott was working the afternoon shift and by 2:00 p.m., he had already started to get ready to go to work. As he picked up his lunch box, and then his coat, I began to feel cramps that were not familiar. I had concerns and so

Scott waited while I called my Obstetrician in London Ontario. After a quick breakdown of my symptoms, my Obstetrician Dr. Matters says, "Well, your due date is tomorrow, so you may as well come to the hospital and get settled in."

I told Scott as he was putting on his shoes to leave. He dropped everything as his eyes got big and his face went a little white. You could see the excitement on his face. I had no idea what to expect but my attitude was more like, "Well, here we go."

He called work to give them the news. The excitement could be heard on the other end of the line. I started to gather my things for the hospital as we prepared for our new arrival.

The drive to London was uneventful, quiet, and peaceful. We arrived at the hospital and walked down the sidewalk toward the Hospital Admissions entrance at St. Joseph Hospital. I was just one step away from the automated doors before they would open when "BAMM!" A contraction so big caused me to grab below my stomach. A nurse saw me and came rushing with a wheelchair. I was grateful to sit down. Once I was admitted, I was led to a room next to the delivery room. As the nurse helped me settle into my bed, I remember looking around thinking to myself. "Well, here I was in the Maternity Ward."

Hours later, the baby was coming, but not fast enough.

As the evening approached, Dr. Matters came for a visit. After an examination, he decided to break my water. Then I walked, and walked and walked. . Scott never left my side, and slept beside me in the hospital chair during the night.

I think the nurses must have changed shifts in the middle of the night because the nurse earlier in the evening was keenly aware of my Obstetrician's warning that he had given during his earlier examination.

"If you feel the baby's head putting too much pressure against your rectum, then he's not coming down and we'll have to do a C-section."

Well, it was inevitable that I would need a C-section because all indications showed that I was too small for a natural birth. However, my built-in tenacity said, "I want to try to do this naturally." So my dear Obstetrician obliged my request. Yet, in the middle of the night, a different nurse came to check on me. I told her, the baby was making it very painful to bare against my rectum. She tossed it off as not being serious.

"Oh, I'm sure it will be fine. You don't have anything to worry about."

I rolled my eyes with a feeling of being ignored. Inside my head I was yelling, "Hello, my doctor said not to let this happen! I'm not very tall you know? Try telling my butt that it will be okay!"

Why does the anesthesiologist have to be cute? I'm a complete mess but here he is standing in front of me. In the early hours of the morning, at about 2 a.m., very carefully, he administers an epidural in my spine. It gives me hope. I'm trusting that it will relieve some pain and pressure that I will feel from the ongoing contractions as the baby moves downward. What I thought would be relief turned out to be the most irritating sensation of pins and needles. As a result, I no longer thought the anesthesiologist was cute!

Scott remained by my side. Although it was a fairly sleepless night, he was wired for sound and driven with anticipation. Dr. Matters enters my hospital room at around 8 a.m. the next morning. A quick examination tells him what he already knows.

"This baby is not coming down so let's get ready for a C-section." He turns to the nurse and nods at her.

At about 10:30 a.m., I am prepped and wheeled into a room and shortly after 11 a.m., the world knows it. Well, at least the Maternity Ward knows it. The loud cries of a little boy could be heard echoing through the halls from the surgical room, while Mom slept off the anesthesia.

Brandon Charles Scott Vincent was born on October 18, 1988. He was right on time, to the very day that he was expected to arrive, weighing eight pounds and four ounces.

Recovering in my room, I realized that I had been placed in a room with other women. No! I had roommates! The one thing that I was looking forward to was some "alone time" after such eventful labor and then surgery too. It wasn't very quiet either. One baby was crying, one mother was talking, another had a boatload of visitors. Another mother was talking to her child, in a voice that sounded like a cartoon character. I rolled my eyes. I just wanted to sleep and perhaps forget about all this for just a little while. I had no space.

It was a strange feeling, very surreal, as I held him for the first time. I've hardly had a chance to know what he looks like due to the foggy feeling from the surgery and drugs to keep the pain low. Although, when I looked at him, I was happy. Some time passed and later that day, my whole family gathered to look at this beautiful little boy. Oh no! My dad brought his camera! Pictures are being snapped here and there. I had no idea what I even looked like. I hadn't seen myself in a mirror for more than 24 hours. Come on people! Really? Please don't take my picture! However, all the fuss over this little boy couldn't be helped. On the day that Brandon was born suddenly, Scott pointed to a double rainbow that could be seen from my hospital window. It was a heavenly moment. I saw it immediately and somehow I knew it was a sign of a double blessing and God's promise to me. We were going to be okay.

Later that day, the nurses are determined to get me up and moving. My head had cleared, but I did not like the sound of what they were suggesting. One nurse attempts to help me out of the bed. The bed had been situated quite high and so I attempted to clumsily slip off the side of the bed, landing with a jolt on my feet. I bent over in pain from the incision being stretched as I wiggled down from the side of the bed. The nurse observed this.

"Oh my, I didn't realize you were *that* short." I looked at her, hoping that daggers weren't flying out of my eyes.

On my second day, I heard other mothers in the room fussing over their babies and talking to them. They made the most ridiculous voices, as I said, like cartoon characters, talking "baby talk" to their newborn babies. I rolled my eyes and turned over. I still just wanted peace and quiet.

On the third day, I was transferred to the Tillsonburg Hospital to continue my recovery. Jesus rose from the grave on the third day, but me? I got transferred to another hospital! Scott and I left St. Joseph Hospital by car. I felt uneasy about the trip home because I didn't feel well. The first night in the hospital proved to be quite alarming for me. I woke up in the middle of the night. I had to go to pee, but I couldn't move my legs. They were dead. I couldn't feel them. I pushed the call button to get a nurse's attention. Instead of coming to my bedside, she spoke with me over the intercom above my bed. I told her I couldn't move my legs and I have to go pee.

"I'm sorry, I'm not able to help you right now. All the nurses are busy delivering babies right now."

"The nerve! Aren't you a nurse?" I thought to myself. "Am I having a bad dream or is this real? Now, what do I do?" After some time, perhaps an hour, the feeling returned to my legs and I was able to go to the washroom.

The next day, I remember drying him off after a bath and observing the build of his little body. His back looked strong and thick. He didn't much appreciate that I delayed dressing him to turn him over and look over his perfect little toes. He began to wail. This prompted me to hurry and get him dressed with the little hospital nighty and wrap him in a warm blanket. At that time, my favorite moment was simply rocking him in the rocking chair next to the hospital bed.

One of the most memorable hospital visits was when Myra came to visit. While I was in high school, this dear lady would come and pick me up on Saturdays and we would go to the church. She played the piano and we would practice songs that I chose. They usually came from an Evie songbook. I was always ready to sing a song at church. She entered the hospital room with a smile. Her gift came in a pretty bag and I felt blessed. Someone thought of me. Among the gifts was a fragrant body powder called, Heaven Scent. It was lovely and smelled so good.

I remained in the hospital for 11 days. This was far longer than expected because my doctor could see that I was not recovering from exhaustion. I had also resisted outwardly revealing all signs of the expected "baby blues". Friends and family visited but I pretended I was okay. I thought that maybe this was how it was supposed to be, but I wanted to be the exception. I wanted to be strong and tough.

Since I wasn't showing signs of typical recovery, physically or emotionally, this gave my doctor a good reason for concern.

I was finally released from the hospital with no change in me, after 11 days.

WINGS TO VICTORY

6 The Journey Begins

As the days progressed with our new baby, I grew less able to cope. Postpartum depression set in. It was an extended season of "baby blues" since it was coupled with a more serious type of depression that can happen after birth known as Postpartum Psychosis. I leaped from a sense of sanity into unpredictable behavior, locking myself in the bedroom and rants of anger and overwhelming tears often. This depression grew in its intensity as time went on. Constant crying followed, pushing bitterness and frustration to the forefront. I also had a feeling of wanting to run away. There were good days and there were bad days. Scott remained strong and supportive, often taking the brunt of random undeserving rants. However, as I continued to develop new physical pain, each emotion increased. This huge deep overwhelming frustration, anxiety, and depression made me feel as though I was out of my mind. People would tell a joke, or say something that warranted laughter or a smile. I knew in my head that I should laugh or smile, but I wasn't sure if this is what was happening on my face. Deep down inside, I felt like the real me was lost. More than anything, I just wanted privacy, yet I didn't want to be alone. I wasn't interested in sharing my feelings. I was suppressing and ignoring my emotions. I was hoping this would make life "normal" or familiar again.

I continued to struggle with pain throughout my shoulders, neck, and lower back that also affected my hips. I was feeling the effects of that work injury since it was not immediately treated when I discovered I was pregnant.

During the pregnancy, I had gained 60 pounds on my small frame. How this happened just snacking on apples, was a mystery to me. Now, here I am struggling with ongoing pain, but I also had a new "self-image" to deal with that I was not so pleased with. Who wants an apron of tummy left from the repercussions of a C-section? I thought to myself, I'll lose the weight and it will be okay. I digress. Let's face it, ladies. I resolved that I would never quite get the old body back. This was hard for me to deal with, not to mention, physically uncomfortable.

While Brandon was just a few weeks old, without

warning, my hips would give out. It was as though they had become detached from my legs. This scared me since it happened many times while holding Brandon in my arms. I sought the doctor's help and learned that I had a spur in my right hip that was causing my hip to "go off track", so to speak, like a train veering off track from the railroad.

It was about this time that Scott developed Carpal Tunnel Syndrome in his wrist due to the repetitive work at the factory. He ended up on Workman's Compensation. It was a blessing for me because I was unable to get up at night with the baby. The cut from the Caesarean would burn. The muscles at the incision would lock and burn, preventing me from lifting myself off of the bed. My hips would not move, becoming stiff at night. Scott would bring Brandon to me and I would nurse him. After approximately 6 weeks, I found that I couldn't emotionally cope with the task of nursing due to all the additional physical pain in my shoulders and neck. At that time, I had to stop and settle for snuggles, laying down with him, which didn't pull on my shoulder and neck.

Some time passed and a routine seemed to set in with the new baby. I resumed involvement at our home church as part of special music occasionally, as well as other activities. However, as much as I tried to keep my emotional instability hidden or subdued, I wasn't always successful at this. I just wanted to believe things were as normal as they could be for me. I just wanted things to go back to normal as I held on to Jesus. I wondered what normal looked like now. A part of me was happy but a part of me felt unsettled and was not coping. Continuing to be involved in music ministry on a local level was a constant sense of stability for me. It gave me a sense of who I was and the things I loved to do as my "mommy" identity became more of a reality. However, I never lost sight of the fact that my love for Jesus was the real reason that I sang.

Oh, I remember our trip to Midland so that Scott's family could finally meet Brandon. Then, we went to Toronto one day. We visited Marilyn and her new husband John. Marilyn was a nurse and John was a Pastor. Oh! Marilyn placed Brandon on her lap and they had a great conversation. He was expressing himself with all kinds of babbling, bright eyes, and smiles. Later, my tooth broke while I had a piece of candy in my mouth. We called the dentist that had worked on that very tooth while we lived in Toronto. Marilyn and John offered us to stay in the guest room overnight so that I could go the next day to the dentist. Well, it was a getaway and actually, it was good for me.

Shortly after, we had a baby dedication at our church for Brandon. The whole family was invited to visit. They stayed overnight at a nearby hotel. The next day, I hosted a full course breakfast and after the service, I had prepared lunch that included homemade lasagna. How did I do that? I loved to host company but I knew it would catch up and I would find myself in pain again.

Each day in the little white house, God had seemed to set us in our own little garden. We discovered some simple pleasures in the little white house on the hill. Peering out the kitchen window we could see little birds, red-wing blackbirds, cardinals, sparrows, house wrens, chipmunks, squirrels, and rabbits, enjoying the gardens and flowering trees. We watched the flowering tulip tree bloom every year from the kitchen window on the north side. We anticipated the lily of the valley flowers that made their grand entrance every Spring, They circled the garden and the house every year. At the very back of the acre property, we found about a dozen apple trees and a wooden fence, that was covered with climbing vines, bursting with fresh berries. I used the fruit in homemade desserts every year. It was a little "land of plenty and promise" for our growing family. These simple pleasures around us were a reminder of God's goodness during my struggle.

In the middle of the night, I would find myself awake, in pain, often with insomnia for several nights in a row, until several nights passed. I would crash and finally sleep through the night. When I found that I couldn't sleep I would revel in the quiet privacy alone on the couch where life seemed to slow down to a complete stop. Although the night was quiet, I quickly became bright-eyed and it seemed that my mind was running a creative marathon as well. I would use that time to focus on conversation with the Lord, reading scripture, writing poetry and songs. The thoughts from my heart, the rich lessons of faith, and words of worship to God lined the lyrics of each song. They told the impact of each step in the journey.

One day, while settling into my daily routine, I propped Brandon up in his bassinet so that he could see me.

After washing up some dishes, I moved around the bassinet in the kitchen to wipe off the stovetop. Suddenly, he stopped me. He was making very loud "cooing" noises, smiling at me and his eyes became round like saucers while his arms waved and his legs kicked with excitement. When I think about this now, I realize that he wasn't fussing at all because he couldn't see me. He was just content to wait there for me. This was one of those moments when I became aware of how much he recognized me and that I meant something to him. I didn't know that I meant anything to him. It was as though he was trying to tell me this. I instantly welled up with tears.

Eventually, intervention from my doctor was very helpful. He still was not aware of how "emotionally stuck" I was and I wasn't about to tell him. I don't know why I didn't want to tell him. Perhaps I was concerned with being labeled. It was only after it had all settled, about a year later, that I told him what I experienced, but for now, I didn't want anyone evaluating me, because I was still unraveling everything in my mind. I was trusting God to help me work out what was going on inside me. I did take my physical concerns to my family doctor. He did arrange an appointment at a hospital where I had a cortisone shot in the hip that was slipping. Relieving this alone, actually changed my outlook. I realized that the physical pain that made me feel completely limited, was like an emotional roadblock. Now that I had pain-free mobility in my hip again, this enabled me to accomplish everyday tasks. I even walked great lengths with the baby in the stroller. At least three times a week I took the opportunity to escape from staring at the walls in the house. I walked a good 45 minutes while pushing a stroller, all the way to the Town Center Mall, where Scott was now Head of Security.

It was during the Summer when Brandon was about eight to ten months old. We spent those afternoons at the mall and I became acquainted with many of the retail employees of the many stores. The association was easy because they all knew my husband, as Head of Mall Security. Brandon charmed them with his cuteness and curly blond hair, entertaining them when business was quiet. This time spent at the mall made my days feel less alone, less unsure of myself and Brandon got to see his dad during work breaks and lunch. After the 45 minute walk to the mall, all the visits, and lunch, I had spent most of the day on my feet there. Now with sore feet, there was no way I was going to walk back too. In the afternoon, I continued browsing through the stores and chatting with store staff, while Brandon had no trouble crashing in the stroller. The end of the day came and Scott finished his shift. We would go home together as a family. Waiting until Scott's shift was over made complete sense. Once we were home, he spent time with Brandon while I started supper. However, that was only if my feet had recovered. Often, we did things as a trio. Scott, me, and the baby.

On one of our routine days at the mall, Brandon and I strolled through the pet store. I thought, "every boy needs a dog". Unaccompanied by my husband, who was unaware of my thoughts, Brandon was just 10 months old. I sat him on the floor in the pet store and with a happy curiosity, he poked the puppy's eyes and tugged on her ears. She didn't seem to mind. She rather enjoyed it. She sat well behaved and wagged her tail, with her tongue eagerly reaching to kiss him as his chubby little fingers poked at her nose. That settled it! When Scott's shift ended, I ushered him into the pet store. He was silent but not mad. I think he was caught off guard, like, "What?" Scott pushed the stroller and I carried a puppy in my arms. We jumped in the car and headed for home.

We named her Coty. She was a beautiful Terrier/Shetland Collie mix with a red-brown tint in her fur and white feather-like fringes of fur on her tail, chest, and neck, with the sweetest and bright brown eyes. She was irresistible. Most of all, Brandon loved her. We watched them grow quickly to be the best of friends.

It was a warm sunny afternoon at home. While tidying up, I happened to glance out the kitchen window next to the back door. My eyes opened wide as I saw several large rodents hiding away in the garden below the window sill. My immediate thought was, "We need a cat!" Shortly afterward, on another afternoon at the mall, I stopped to "browse" at the pet store. My eyes glanced at the litter and I picked a beautiful kitten with Tortious-shell and-Tabby mix markings from the litter. We called her Tessa. She turned out to be quite the snuggle bug, crawling on my lap for her afternoon naps. A few weeks later, she went missing. I couldn't find her anywhere in the house. Concerned that she escaped outside, I was unsure that she was ready to explore the great outdoors. I assumed she was lost and gone for good. I knew the main objective was that we needed a cat to keep a rodent issue at bay. The mere scent of a cat can send rodents looking for new territory. That afternoon I set Brandon up in the stroller, packed up the diaper bag, and went to the mall. My goal was to see if there were any new litter of kittens at the pet store. When I arrived, I looked in the cage. There sat one little kitten. She was the funniest-looking thing I'd ever seen. She looked part alien with her super large ears, buggy green-yellow eyes, and tiny pink nose. Her fur was a pretty soft blue-grey with a tuxedo of white that stretched from her belly and came to a point over the top of her nose. Her strange-shaped head was amusing and I figured well, I'll take the "unlovely one". I named her Rosie because of her cute pink nose.

Scott asked me what happened to Tessa and I told him, "I can't find her. I think she got outside by mistake and can't find her way home."

My husband never grew up with pets in his childhood home, except several goldfish and a hamster. He claimed that he managed to drive each one of them to a quick death. Strangely enough, he never said a word about our growing family of fur babies. At the end of his shift, we all went home together, with a new kitty too.

I held Rosie in my arms as we tumbled through the door with the baby, stroller, and other packages. I stopped in my tracks, completely surprised at what I saw before me. As I held Rosie in my arms, Tessa, with a sleepy look on her face, came strolling out of the storage room from behind the kitchen. "Oh-oh!"

Two kittens later and a puppy, I had my hands full, but that was okay. Over time, it became obvious that Tessa preferred to attack whatever dangled over her head. This did not make her a mouser. She was more like a fly-catcher, but together, their presence did scare the brood of rodents away eventually. Rosie's rare beauty was revealed later as she turned out to be a mix of an Asian and domestic breed. She grew into her big ears and buggy eyes quite beautifully and took on the most elegant stature. Tessa's nose was a little out of joint upon Rosie's arrival and she no longer wanted long cuddles, but Rosie was by my side all the time. She turned out to be quite the mouse catcher, "bringing home the bacon" and leaving it on the front step. It was a clear token of love and affection as a productive member of the family, but gross!

While cleaning up in the kitchen one day, I heard Brandon laughing so hard. Of course, by this time, he was crawling and so I was diligent to keep him in my line of sight. I turned around and discovered our dog Coty on the floor with Brandon, tickling his ribs with her nose and then licking his face. I laughed as I thought this was the sweetest thing. Coty became Brandon's best buddy with regular wrestling and tickling matches on the floor. The animals were good for our family. They brought laughter and entertainment, and we enjoyed interacting with them.

WINGS TO VICTORY

7 Awakened

Little did I know that the summer days spent at the mall would make way for new steps to healing. As the Autumn days started to settle in, on another day, I meandered through the mall while Brandon had a nap in the stroller. There at the end of the corridor was a table with a display of literature. Booklets and brochures about babies and the development of life were spread over the table and a few ladies stood behind it. They were from the local Right To Life organization. I had a brief conversation with one of them and was encouraged to take home a little booklet.

The booklet was about family and it contained very touching photos of mothers and babies together. As a four-year art student, I was visually inspired by the images in this booklet. At this time, I was still suffering from depression but even so, the pictures stirred my soul. After dinner that evening, I took an art pad and pencil and sat down at one end of the couch to draw. Sometimes I would draw all day and into the evening. My husband gave me all the time that I needed to "let go". I stowed away to draw, as he cared for Brandon.

My dad was doing a fair bit of freelance photography at this time. He had acquired some very specialized and professional camera equipment and had an eye for taking great pictures. I had recently received copies of some wonderful candid photos of Brandon that my dad had photographed. I knew he was beautiful from the time I first saw him, but after a while, I never paid much attention because my world became full of distractions with physical and emotional pain. I had never quite noticed how he was growing to be much more adorable every day until I saw these photos.

I loved the vibrant color of these pictures that showed his beautiful face. His bright eyes and pink cheeks with the little curl in his lips looked "handcrafted". I sat at the end of the couch and drew detailed sketches of him from these pictures. As I studied his sweet spirit the beautiful curves of his face, came through the pictures. It brought me healing and I finally realized that I was connecting with him.

My husband continued to take care of Brandon and the house, as I sat there and drew pictures every day. He realized that I needed to do this to reacquaint myself with who I am and the things I once enjoyed.

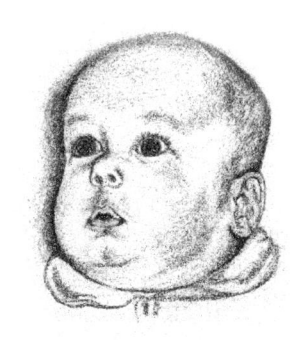

I had once felt as though my life's calling as mother, wife, singer, and artist were all compartmentalized. Now I was beginning to feel those parts of my life beginning to blend into one, with balance.

When Brandon turned one year old, I was doing better and started to feel like myself emotionally but now I was nearly three months pregnant with our second child. If you're asking why we would have another baby so close to the first one when I was having such a hard time, well . . . that was God's plan, not mine. To this day, we still blame it on the Strawberry pie after dinner one evening! This pregnancy was easier and by this time, we were running a very successful janitorial business. I was working in the business and staying in shape and eating well. It was a good pregnancy, however during the last 2 months, I was hospitalized twice for several weeks each time. There were signs of early labor and I was ordered on bed rest. My doctor knew that bed rest would be hard with a little toddler at home and so he admitted me to the hospital. Baby number two was fine, as long as the baby came on time.

I was released from the hospital as my due date approached. This would be my final visit to see my family doctor before the baby was born. Since we knew already, "do not stop for labor, go directly to C-section", my doctor discussed scheduling me to be admitted to the hospital in town, on the due date. He told me the date would be April 26th. I didn't like this number. It meant that the baby would be born close to the weekend and so I asked if we could schedule it for the 24th. This way my husband got the week off work. I know this was kind of silly, but I preferred the number 24.

My doctor shrugged his shoulders and said, "Sure".

It was a day like any other day in the Spring. The day started as usual and was uneventful, with the exception that today was the day for baby number two. Kyle Roland Joseph Vincent was born April 24th, weighing 7

pounds, 11 oz. Another Caesarean and once again, I was in the hospital longer than expected, a total of 14 days.

After the surgery, I did not want to see Kyle. I felt numb. I didn't know how I was going to handle this. On that first day, I could only feel the pain and hated that I had to go through this. It all changed when my nurse came to me later. She offered to rub some cream on my back and then told me how beautiful my baby boy was. Her face expressed such a genuine heart when she told me that he was absolutely beautiful.

"He is one of the most beautiful babies that I've ever seen." Then she asked me, "Are you ready to see him?"

I agreed because I knew it would be terrible if I said no. She left my room and returned a few minutes later with Kyle in her arms. When she placed him in my arms.

"See? Isn't he just beautiful?"

I touched his little hand and gasped, amazed as I watched him instantly curl his little hand around my baby finger. I felt as though he instantly recognized me. Had I realized what I was missing then I wouldn't have held back so much? This was my most memorable moment with Kyle when we finally met face to face.

The slow recovery due to burning pain and exhaustion continued through my body but my hope was gaining momentum. After months of settling in with our newest little one, I was beginning to explore ministry opportunities. It was around this time that I became involved with the Right to Life Committee in town. It started when I presented the sketches to them that I had done. Eventually, the sketches were printed on note cards and used to raise funds for the local Right to Life organization. About a year later, I was appointed Vice President and then President of the local Right to Life. I shortened my term as President when I stepped down due to personal ministry obligations. However, it was a wonderful experience for me.

Spontaneously, on a trip to London one day, we stopped in to visit Bob and Diana. Bob's passion was to sing and play his guitar. He had written some great songs too. Both of them were involved in ministry. We were warmly welcomed and they offered us a seat on their big comfy couch. Even still, I sat down very gingerly. Early in my first pregnancy, the bruised tailbone that I suffered after a fall down the stairs was still, shall we say, my bone of contention. It had been over a year and it was still no better.

There was a sense of excitement and awe in Bob's voice as he began to share about a video he had seen. It was a live recording of Jeff Fenholt singing the song "Majesty", and apparently, people were being healed as he sang the song. Jeff Fenholt was a part of the secular group "Black Sabbath" until he became a believer and received salvation.

Bob turned on the video while Diane offered us a Twinkie roll. As we started opening the wrapper on the Twinkie roll, we heard Jeff begin to sing the song "Majesty". People were lined up as he walked past them, touching them to pray. His voice sounded strong and bold, almost as though he was in warfare. The intensity of his voice and the power that I could sense engaged me so much that I could see nothing around me. I took a bite of my Twinkie, but my eyes never left the television screen. Suddenly, without warning, I felt a warm sensation on my tailbone. As quickly as I noticed the warmth, 2 seconds later, the pain in my tailbone left. I was completely free from pain in my tailbone.

A look of surprise and amazement came over my face. "My tailbone! I just felt my tailbone get warm and the pain is gone."

"Wow! That's awesome!" Bob quickly responded.

We all became overwhelmed and amazed at what God had done. It didn't matter that we were eating Twinkies. It didn't matter that we were just watching a recording of an earlier broadcast. It didn't matter that it was on TV. God did it!

One day a phone call came from a lady named Betty. She and her husband ran a trailer camp a little way out of town. I have no idea to this day how she found out about me but she asked me if I would sing at their Sunday service on the campgrounds. I agreed and then she asked me, "Can you do something for the children too?" I willingly agreed and as a result, God inspired my creativity and imagination. A puppet stage was made from an old refrigerator cardboard box. I painted it bright colors and created one puppet with supplies that I found at the local craft store. It was just a few doors down from where we lived, in the basement of a lady's house. I picked items that drew my eye and inspired me. I had no idea what I was making until I saw it start to take shape as I was making it. The puppet turned out to be a shaggy dog. Of course, we called him, "Shaggy"! How original! Over time, Scott and I developed a ministry to children called "The King's Court". I invested in puppet construction courses, bought a sewing machine and we bought a sound system. I wrote original object lessons, stories, and songs as well as designed more custom puppets and a new puppet stage.

We had lots of help from family who were there to engineer and paint the three-sided puppet stage. It was made of three wood panels and piano hinges. It wasn't long before we were beginning to get calls from churches across Ontario Canada to do Vacation Bible Schools and special presentations for children. In addition, I was invited to sing during church services. We were booked on an average of 36 bookings just for Sunday School and children's ministry alone from May to November each year. We did this for many years, while Brandon and his brother Kyle came with us. We always ensured that there was a mom or two that could look after the boys while we did Children's ministry.

Shaggy turned out to be a hit from his very first appearance at that small little Children's Church at camp. One child asked if he could hug Shaggy and so Scott stayed behind the puppet stage holding up Shaggy for a hug. More children followed, just to hug Shaggy. Scott and I laughed about it later, marveling at the Children's response.

While I still suffered from fatigue and pain throughout my body, it had minimized. I somehow think that this creative purpose and call was a huge distraction and gave me the drive to keep going. I still took it slowly and I carefully chose my tasks. My dear husband never missed an opportunity to make things easier for me. I look back now and wonder if people ever thought he was my slave? The beauty in this journey was the glimmer of hope and real miracles that I experienced along the way.

We had a baby dedication at our church for Kyle too. The same opportunity presented itself and family joined to celebrate. Once again, I enjoyed hosting family and made an array of fancy sandwiches, and salads. Scott helped me in the kitchen and it was wonderful to have the company.

It was about the time that my sister Paula was in the planning stages of her wedding. I was her Maid of Honor. After Kyle's birth, I was making some effort to lose a little weight before the big day. Just down the street, a new weight-loss clinic had moved into a small mall down the street. They sold pre-packaged food with their program. This sounded like an easy solution for a busy mom like me and so I decided to give it a try. It was about 6 weeks into the program when I developed excruciating pain on the left side of my ribs. I buckled over in pain with several episodes in a row over the following days. A trip to the doctor was in order and after some tests, the results were in. The doctor wanted to schedule me for surgery to remove my gallbladder. SURGERY??!! NO! Just hearing the word "surgery" was overwhelming and traumatic for me after two C-sections and the aftermath that I was still feeling.

I laid in bed, while the house was quiet that night. Scott was asleep beside me. From the deepest part of me, trying not to wake him, I cried out with the loudest voice I could, in my head. The tears flowed and my pillow was wet. I can't deny, I felt fear, but mostly I felt traumatized. The thoughts in my head were loud as I protested with great distress, "I can't handle another surgery Lord. Please don't let this happen. Please no, I can't do it. I'll snap. It's just more than I can handle. I can't handle going under the knife again. Please take this away." At that moment, I felt a little bubble on the left side of my ribs. Suddenly, I felt a series of them pop, like skipping stones on the water. I felt peace and surprise all at once. It caught my breath for a mere second, then I wiped my tears away and flipped over my pillow. This peace he gave me, quickly caused me to fall into a restful sleep. He truly heard my cry and delivered me. I never had a gallbladder attack again, and so I never followed through with the surgery. I did tell Scott the next day but at that time in my life, I never talked to the doctor because I didn't want to hear any negative or doubtful interrogations from him. Since I had every evidence to believe I was healed, I just knew that I knew, that Jesus had taken care of this. That's all that mattered.

On another day in the evening, the phone rang and it was my friend Sandra from Toronto. Sandra was also a Gospel singer-songwriter. It was a few years prior when she had discovered my ministry flyer at an event she was attending. My flyer prompted her to call me and that first phone call sparked a friendship. Since then, we have talked many times on the phone and had also visited together at her home a few times. During this particular phone call, I shared one of the songs that the Lord had given me on a sleepless night. Sandra encouraged me saying, "Laurie, people need to hear these songs! They will minister to them and you should consider recording them."

I remember thinking, "But I'm a mess!"

I took her words to heart and tucked them away, in God's hands.

LAURIE MARKS VINCENT

8 Lions And Trumpets

It became more and more frequent that God would speak to me through dreams. In one of my dreams, I was on a road trip with my mother and sister. We stopped at a hotel to stay for the night. We were led down a set of stairs and through a hallway, each made of cobble-like flat flagstones. It was apparent that we were going down, not up. The room was large with only two beds in it. The first thing that my Mother did was use the bathroom. The door was open and I noticed that water was running in the tub. There was no one there to turn the water on and my Mother never even acknowledged that the water was running. As the water filled the tub, I stood in the doorway and noticed that it reached the top of the tub but it did not overflow. I then saw that the water continued to rise as though there was an invisible wall of glass in front of the tub. As the water rose, I could see the pipes behind the shower wall being exposed through the wall.

I spoke up and said to my mother, "There is something wrong. We need to leave this place."

She assured me that we would be fine here and then without her knowledge, she began levitating. Something unusual and dark was going on. I started to press, "No we have to leave now!"

Realizing that she was oblivious to what I saw, I began to yell out the name of Jesus. At that moment, I couldn't breathe and felt as though my lungs were being pressed down on with a heavy weight. As I continued gasping for air, I woke up from the dream and opened my eyes. At that instant, I saw the head of an ugly old woman hovering over my body, and yet her body stood on its own, at my bedside. I quickly reached in desperation for my husband, with one hand, hitting him to wake him. I couldn't speak, I was choking, but he felt my hand hit his side. Although he couldn't see what I was seeing, he was instantly aware of what was happening. He immediately knew that this was spiritual. He quickly sat up and spoke out boldly "In the name of Jesus, Satan I rebuke you!"

Immediately, there was a relief. I gasped for air and began to breathe. The entity was instantly gone. I later came to a full understanding of what God was revealing to me through this dream.

There had been some strange experiences in the little white house lately. At the time, I didn't know for sure if the house was "haunted" or if I was being hunted. Perhaps it was just my imagination. I thought I was simply paranoid.

I'm not one to look for a reason to blame the enemy forces. I don't like to give them too much credit, but we must recognize enemy opposition in our lives. I guess this was boot camp for me.

Scott was still working the afternoon shift. I was often on red alert during the late nights alone, in the little white house, located on a hill, somewhat isolated at the end of town. Occasionally, Coty would bark if she felt the need, but usually, she was snuggled up at the end of one of the boy's beds at night. On one particular night, she did bark and I sensed there was a need to be cautioned. I prayed and then my attention was directed to the window on the north side of the living room. It was dark outside. There was no outside light to cast on our property except the street light in the front yard. I could see nothing from where I stood. I closed the curtains and went to bed. Needless to say, I was a little on edge and it was not a good night's sleep.

The next morning I walked the property on the north side of the house. I looked around the flower garden that stretched the length of the house but could see nothing unusual. It wasn't until I reached the front of the garden near the side of the road, that I noticed something of concern. Only steps away from the road, there was a very large mature tree at the front of the garden. Its foliage spread over a vast amount of the garden and hung quite low to the ground. Directly under the lowest branches, there was an area of long grass that had been flattened and had left the impression in the shape of a person's body. I could only assume that Coty had barked because she was aware that someone was outside the house. Perhaps it was a hitchhiker traveling out of town, but I felt affirmed that day. It was good to know that the Holy Spirit truly led me to the window that night after I had prayed. Perhaps there was never any danger at all, but I will never know because I had prayed for divine protection specifically on that night.

Late one evening, I sat at the dining room table while Scott was working. The boys had already been asleep for quite some time. Papers were scattered around me as I was planning for a Children's Ministry engagement that weekend. I was sorting out my thoughts and the order of the children's lesson when I looked up. My eyes caught the glaring stare of something evil. It was looking at me, eyes piercing, in the dining room window. Was I hallucinating? I was not sure what I was looking at, but I was moved to my feet and ran to the telephone. Not once at all did I fear for the boys who were safely sleeping in their beds. I quickly called my friend Nancy on the phone. Nancy had been a friend and confidante during difficult times in my life before I had even met Scott. Her sister Julia was also my friend but our friendship was different. I gleaned wisdom and understanding of spiritual things from the Word of God when Nancy and I talked. Little did either one of us realize, but she helped me make some sense of the mess, at that time in my life. She was currently living in Tulsa Oklahoma.

She answered the phone, and in my desperation, I am sure I sounded a bit frantic. I told her what I saw and Nancy began to pray with me. As she was praying, God allowed me to hear something in the spirit realm. I heard the sound of voices like trumpets, blasting with one long note, sounding off in the distance. The sound of the voices was like trumpets. They had a strong but ominous presence. Then I heard another group of voices like trumpets blend with the first voices, in a harmonizing note. Then a third note harmonized over the first two notes. The notes did not stop and then start again to take a breath. They just kept on blaring. Just as Nancy finished praying, they stopped. Peace entered the room. Whatever the battle was, it was already won in the heavens, by the sound of voices like trumpets that blew it down, like the Jericho walls.

Around this time, I was recording my second album, making trips back and forth to a studio in London, Ontario Canada. This is back when cassettes were the "in" thing. The songs on the recording were ones that I had written during those late nights after Brandon was born. By now, I had become quite prolific in this skill, working with a music arranger, who only lived a few doors down from us. It was after the recording was done that the Fibromyalgia and Chronic Fatigue, yet undiagnosed, kicked back into high gear. The CD was entitled "When You Reached In My Heart". Although I never really got things off the ground, when the recording was done, it was well-received on a local level in the region.

As time went by, many doctor visits and medical tests ended with no answers and many nights were still spent writing new songs, and intimately talking with God throughout the struggle. This went on for months which turned into years, and then Brandon started Junior Kindergarten. I do remember that I rarely had a phone call from anyone. People always seemed to be busy. It's not that I didn't have anything to keep myself busy. It's simply that I was looking for some adult conversation and a few different faces to look at.

I was a diligent homemaker. The house hardly ever had anything out of place and I hated clutter. Even when the boys played, it was organized and contained to one area. There was one day when I had just finished some dusting and vacuuming. The boys were playing in their bedroom. While Kyle was busy building a tower of blocks, Brandon was passing time with little cars on his bed. He used his blankets to make hills and roads and then moved the cars over the imaginary hills and valleys. I had seen him do it many times before. At the end of Brandon's bed, there was a window that was about 2 feet wide and 4 feet tall. I had retired to the couch in the living room once the vacuuming was done and was now watching a television program. I was startled when I saw Brandon running out of his bedroom with a look of fright on his face. His little feet were carrying him as swiftly as he could go.

"Mommy! Mommy!" He came to my side and I quickly sat him beside me on the couch.

"What's the matter, Brandon?"

"A lion came to my window and said he said he was going to eat me!"

I calmed him down for a minute, holding him close to my side. I pondered what he had just described, recalling the scripture verse, "The enemy goes about as a roaring lion, seeking whom he may devour." [1 Peter 5:8] I knew what this scripture meant but at the time, I couldn't see the future. Once Brandon seemed to be calm, I asked him, "Brandon, what happened to the lion?" I was amazed at his response.

"A man with "lellow" (yellow) hair came and pulled him by his feet and threw him across the yard."

Had Brandon heard the enemy's threat and seen an angel come to his defense? I think so. I can't see any other logical explanation that correlates with his story.

It was the year after Brandon finished Junior Kindergarten that we reluctantly moved out of the little white house on the hill. This was because the owner had passed away and her possessions were being divided and sold. We moved into a townhouse and found that this was a real change for us but conveniently it was also just down the road from Brandon's new school. I could feel the pressure of change. Adjusting was hard and not without great personal upheaval and frustration, but I did it.

I remember after a long day, unpacking the boxes and setting up our home, we were so exhausted. We had gone in and out of the back door, dumping empty boxes and purging what we could, all day long. I had followed Scott up the stairs to head to bed. After I finished in the bathroom, I came to bed and discovered Scott was already asleep. I crawled into bed and had only laid my head on the pillow.

I heard the words in my head, "Did you lock the back door?"

Alarmed, I quickly went down two short flights of stairs to the back door. As I approached the back door, I saw that it was cracked open by about four inches. As I laid my hand on the doorknob, my eyes caught a young man tip-toeing to our back door. He was only about 4 feet away from the door. I was not afraid. I simply shut the door firmly, to let him know I saw him, then locked the door. It was good that I heeded the alarm in my head. These little moments are quite likely the Holy Spirit giving us these thoughts to protect and guide us. They should never be ignored, but always explored.

There were some days when I would be flooded with emotion that brought me to tears and there was no reason except for a feeling of being trapped. One day, while washing dishes at the kitchen sink, overwhelming desperation came over me. As tears ran down my face I decided that I was going to have to find the reason for these outbursts. Brandon was in grade one and Kyle was in Junior Kindergarten and so I had the house to myself during the day with the freedom to do what I wanted. This made no sense! I couldn't even put a finger on why I was crying. This was a real frustration. Honestly, if I never existed, that would have been easier. I loved my family too much and so doing away with my life was only a thought. I only wanted to stop the pain, not my life. In desperation, I searched for the phone number of a Christian counselor in the nearest city. While tears ran down my face, I spoke with a lady on the phone, who was very understanding. The conversation lasted for less than 10 minutes when she spoke the very words that propelled me forward. Her voice was loving but strong as she advised me.

"Laurie, whatever it is that is causing this, it's inside of you and has to come out and be revealed. Ask the Lord to show you and then surrender it to Him."

That night I prayed a simple prayer of few words.

"Lord, by your Holy Spirit, please counsel me in my sleep. Please be my counselor."

Revealing my deepest personal secrets made me feel weak if I talked with another human being. However, I knew that if the Lord intervened and showed me, I wouldn't resist. If he visited me in my sleep I would be vulnerable and receptive. That very same night I had a series of dreams that spoke to my spirit and the depth of my soul.

In the first dream, I hear our dog Coty asking to go outside. As I lead her to the back door, I go down a short flight of stairs to the main floor. I reached the bottom of the stairs and took a few steps toward the door. When I turned to look back at Coty, instead I saw an image of myself coming down the stairs. This image of me was everything that I wished I could be. A little taller, and a little thinner. My hairstyle was "just so", only a little longer. In my reality, I regretted recently getting my hair trimmed. In the dream, I was wearing the clothes that I had laid eyes on at a store earlier that week, which I had regretted not purchasing. When this image of myself reached the bottom of the stairs, I realized that it had no face. There was an empty dark hole where my face should be, surrounded by my hair. The "real me" in the dream stood there puzzled. Suddenly, I was cautioned as the image of myself came toward me. It stretched out its arms with its hands reaching for my throat. Frightened by my faceless double approaching me, I found myself cornered in the room with nowhere to go. I began to struggle, gasp for air, screamed, and tried to get away. I was startled in my sleep, the dream stopped, and yet I continued to sleep.

The second dream began. I found myself back in the house that I grew up in as a teenager. While I was in the kitchen cleaning up after supper, my parents were getting dressed. That evening, they were going out to a fancy event, and as the oldest of the four children, I often babysat the younger ones. In this dream, I was wearing a new blue jean skirt that belonged to my mom. Sharing some of the things in her closet was something my mom often did with me as I grew older and she still does to this day.

In the dream, my dad came into the kitchen and glanced at me. He then spoke as though he was slightly annoyed.

"What are you doing wearing your Mother's new skirt?"

My Mom quickly jumped in, hollering from the other room. "It's okay, I told her that she could wear it."

"Oh okay." My dad nodded. I continued cleaning up the kitchen as my parents were nearly ready to parade out the door for the evening.

"It's time to go." said my dad, and my mom followed

him as she picked up her purse and an evening shawl.

I followed behind to say goodbye and close the door, then my mom turned around and wrapped her left arm around my neck, and whispered in my ear.

"I want you to know that I appreciate you." The dream ended there as early morning approached.

At that moment, I woke up laying in the fetal position on my side. Scott had already left for work and so I was alone. I quickly became aware that my left ear was moist as though someone had been breathing heavily and whispering very close, as my mother did in the dream. In an instant, I sensed the majestic, loving, and nurturing presence of the great I AM, sitting on the edge of the bed, at my belly. Although I instantly recognized God's presence, I quickly rose out of bed, not knowing what to do with what had just happened. By the time I reached the end of the bed, I felt emotion well up inside of me and I tumbled to the floor, in tears.

I knew that God had caused these dreams to bring several emotions to the surface that I had not recognized or even acknowledged. This was about my regrets, wishes, disappointments in how God made me and how I felt "less". In many cases, I had put these emotions aside. I ignored them and suppressed them when certain incidents happened in the past. It was a coping mechanism not to "feel". This very moment was instant healing for me. Suddenly, I was the butterfly and my cocoon had just started to break open. I was able to see a sliver of light pierce through the cocoon.

9

A Change of Space

Due to poor staff performance, we lost our janitorial business despite endeavoring to manage the staff. We would be unaware that a night of work was not done and contracts started to close down on us. It was impossible to go away on a family trip because we had to "babysit" staff or cover for them. It was overwhelming to see a thriving business that we had worked so hard to grow, being torn down. In addition, it was a great source of financial backing for the ministry. As a result, my husband was once again working at a factory during the day and attempting to keep the janitorial business going in the evenings.

By 1996 the loss of the thriving janitorial business,

which funded the ministry was behind us. We never thought of asking for donations because we didn't have charitable status at that time. We were trusting God for a financial miracle for the ministry. At that time, we were left with a stalled, broken-down vehicle that once towed the ministry trailer. It was apparent that what seemed a very "in demand" children's ministry, was finished since we no longer had a vehicle suitable for towing the ministry trailer. The new car that we were able to purchase would not handle the load. I continued music ministry as I was able to but there was no more Children's ministry. There were still a few small janitorial contracts that remained, but the big contracts that supported the music and children's ministry were gone. It was shortly after, that filing for bankruptcy was evident.

Later on, with Scott's job secured, we had a breakthrough when a private deal came to our attention. An opportunity to "rent to own" a house had presented itself to us. We signed a two-year "lease to own" contract and moved into a newly built beautiful brick house that was moderate in size. We hoped to put our rent credits toward a down payment in the future.

A year in the new house and we had decorated with a "down to earth" sophistication. I had made custom curtains for the dining room and enjoyed the steely blue and warm corals as accents. We regularly filled the house with friends and family. The bonus family room in the basement had an additional bedroom and a full bathroom. It worked out perfect for when guests came to stay. It was especially cozy for Scott's mother who came to visit from Midland Ontario.

This house had light in it and I had found new healing and freedom. My mind seemed free and I had found a deeper intimacy in Christ.

The Lord had opened my spirit, healed some soul wounds, but my body still hurt. The boy's school was five blocks away and the walk there and back each morning always left me with sore muscles, no matter how often I walked the short 10-minute route with them. After several months of walking the same route, my muscles should have adjusted but they didn't. However, this didn't change my heart's desires and new songs continued to flood through me, not just in the late night but now, they came during the day too.

Where I once found myself standing at the kitchen sink crying, in deep despair, I now stood at my kitchen sink in my new house and heard the Spirit of God speak to me. The chore of washing the dishes was made so pleasurable beyond my wildest dreams, because of His tangible and constant presence with me. One day, as I was washing the dishes and sharing with God what was on my heart. I felt his presence cover me heavily and very quickly. His presence was so strong that I could barely stand. I quickly left the dishes and almost stumbled over to the living room. Bent over, landing on my knees and overwhelmed by the strength of his power, I heard music pour into my mind along with words. I dropped to the floor on my knees, finding myself in the corner of the living room. Grabbing my notebook and pen, it seemed as though the words poured out like water. I wrote the song "Under the Shadow" in a matter of 10 minutes. This experience left me in tears and joy I can't explain.

I knew that he was telling me that I was "Under the Shadow of Your Wings", just as the words to the song were written. Up until this time, of all the songs I had ever written, never had this ever happened to me. Never before, had I ever experienced God giving me a song in this way.

"Under The Shadow"

Under The Shadow of Your Wings, I will praise You.
I lift my voice to you and sing.
Here in your presence, I will stay,
when the light has left my day.
Just to know that you are with me,
Under the Shadow of Your Wings

Under the Shadow of Your Wings, You will keep me.
I can be sure of just one thing.
You go before me in the fall,
when the enemy builds his wall
Just to know that You are with me,
Under the Shadow of Your Wings

And I've searched for strength to fly,
and given up when the tide was high

> Now I've learned I can be stronger,
> when I walk through it with you Lord,
> and hold on.... hold on
> *(repeat first verse)*

Words and Music Laurie Marks Vincent

© Copyright Laurie Marks Vincent SOCAN BMI

At this point in my life, I had never connected the context directly with Psalm 91. I discovered years later that these lyrics were based on Psalm 91:1.

"One who lives in the shelter of the Most High will stay in the shadow of the Almighty."

This song was released on two of my recordings "When You Reached In My Heart" as well as the CD, "Love So Amazing" (2004). At the time, this second CD wasn't even an idea on my mind at all. It was during our stay in this house that my recording, "When You Reached In My Heart", was completed and released on cassette locally in the region. My friend Sandra also eventually recorded the song on her CD years later.

We also made good friends with a young couple who lived next door to us. We would visit them, play cards and just chat with them. We'll call them John and Amy. They enjoyed interacting with our little boys but they had no children of their own. The friendship began to deepen one day when we learned that there was some sad news. They were longing to have a child, but they learned that they couldn't. I saw the pain on Amy's face every time she struggled with endometriosis. It seemed that the most important thing for them was to move on from this. We continued to encourage each other in decorating decisions inside and outside of the house. It seemed to be our common thread.

Sadly, when we moved into this new house, the deal was that we were not allowed to take Coty with us. I watched Brandon mourn, missing his dog every day. He taped a picture of Coty to his wall right beside his pillow, crying himself to sleep many times. An elderly gentleman and his daughter gladly took Coty. They lived in the country and it was a good place for her because she loved to run in the wide-open spaces. I don't remember how we connected again but we did find out that Coty had puppies. We later visited them and got to spend some time with Coty. She was happy and seemed to recognize us. It was a good day, especially for Brandon and that made me happy too.

It was heartbreaking that we could not keep Coty and I should have realized then that Brandon's broken heart was just a sign that we would not only lose Coty but lose the house too. As the two-year term on the new house drew to an end, it was time to proceed with the purchase of this new house that we had "rented to own". This was new and we were young, so we failed to realize that we should have consulted with our lawyer when we signed the "lease to own" contract. We were caught in a clause that made the purchase impossible. After a consultation with our lawyer, who was familiar with the seller's "dirty deeds and scams", we learned that we had lost what we understood to be "monetary credits" and now we had no means to purchase the house. We left the house with no other recourse, a loss of ten thousand dollars, and moved into a tiny two-bedroom apartment.

The apartment was nice and clean but very small. It was on the main floor, on the corner, in the front of the building. The location was very convenient for the boys to go in and out through the patio door to play with their friends. Both cats, Tessa and Rosie were still with us when we moved there. . We spent a few years in that apartment, and during that time, some amazing things happen.

The patio door became an escape route for Tessa, who was an indoor cat up until this point. She had a nighttime suitor. He was a handsome cat with long hair, beautiful markings, and such a handsome face. He would spend evenings at our patio door watching for her. She would cry and pace the floor at the patio door, asking to go out, and so we let her go. She came back every time. Then one day, as she was just laying next to me, I saw her tummy move, like there was a little ball inside her. I felt her tummy and discovered the little ball, moving, living, and kicking. Tessa was pregnant.

When the time came, Tessa had some trouble but with the guidance of our vet, over the phone, we were able to help her. She gave birth to one sweet little female kitty that was practically a carbon copy of her. Tessa chose to keep her baby in the boy's bedroom. We set up a cozy box for her nursery. One day as I was tidying up, I heard the sound of the kitten crying but she wasn't in her box. I traced her cry and discovered that Tessa had put her baby in Kyle's bottom dresser drawer. I called Tessa and showed her that I put her baby back in the box. She jumped in the box with her. I told Kyle when he came home from school. He had a grin on his face and thought that was pretty special that she chose his dresser drawer. We kept her baby and called her "Alley". Now we had three cats.

For a few years now I had been the coordinator for the Gospel Music Stage on Canada Day in Tillsonburg. All over the downtown core, there were stages and displays of interest and celebration. I had written a song called "Canada Our Country" that year and invited some regional Christian artists to spend the day together, to participate in the Gospel Music Stage. Together, at a pre-set time, we would sing "Canada Our Country". Musicians and singers from as far as Toronto came to the little town of Tillsonburg for the occasion. Sandra was there too. I was blessed that they were willing to come.

That particular year I sent out a poster to all the churches in the town and announced that there would be a time dedicated to praying for our country, at 2:00 p.m. on Canada Day.

The music began at the Gospel Music Stage and people arrived, perching themselves on lawn chairs and blankets in front of the stage, in the park grass. People who lived in nearby buildings came out on their balconies to listen.

To my delight, at 2:00 p.m. the crowd began to swell. I was so happy to see such a great response from the churches in the town. We prayed for our country and then together with the music artists, began to sing the feature song "Canada Our Country". As we sang the song, people started to notice a cloud in the sky that stood out among the rest. This cloud seemed to be riding on its own gust of gentle wind that separated it from the other clouds. It was hanging much lower than the rest of the clouds in the sky and headed right for us. The cloud beamed from the inside out with a pure brilliance rivaling any other rainbow. The colors seem to rotate inside of the cloud as though they were alive. It settled in one place in the sky and stayed hovering over the audience. It's as though it had joined the crowd while we continued singing. By the time the song had finished, every artist on the stage had noticed this cloud. People in the crowd were pointing to the cloud, marveling at its peculiar and beautiful appearance. What could this have possibly been? A cloud that looked like a cloud but did not behave like a cloud? I believe that on that Canada Day, July 1st, the presence of God had shown Himself. He physically visited us in a cloud that day. He was showing us that he honored our prayer and was pleased with our efforts to love and pray for our country. The thought also crossed my mind that He just wanted to come to join the crowd, to be among His people who were together from different churches. Maybe it was all of these reasons together, but it reminded me of the story in Exodus 13 when God led the people by a cloud during the day and a pillar of fire by night. He was certainly with his people.

Every time that I managed and participated in a ministry event I needed to rest the day before because I needed my strength the next day. The day after was usually a "write-off" for me, filled with fatigue, lack of drive, and pain. Still struggling with pain and fatigue I continued with music ministry and continued to try and find an answer as to why I was in this physical pain. The biggest frustration was the constant feeling of "running out of steam" with exhaustion. Once exhaustion set in, depression seemed to follow. I had not been diagnosed with Fibromyalgia yet. At that time, Fibromyalgia was considered a suspicious unfounded syndrome, possibly all in one's head, according to the medical community.

I spent my mornings rotating between television programs such as, "Joyce Meyer", "Believer's Voice of Victory", "James Robison", "One Hundred Huntley Street" and "I Love Lucy". I drew the truth from these programs that ministered to me. I was also not in the habit of eating breakfast and my common sense knew this was important and so I promised myself and God that I would change this.

There were many mornings, as I sat down to watch these programs, I would eat a banana or grab another piece of fruit. It was the easiest way to have breakfast without much effort. I didn't have to cook and I liked it that way when I didn't feel physically strong. It was about a month after I had started this love affair in God's Word with the television in the mornings, that I discovered the depression was lifting. It was the mixture of laughter (crazy Lucy and Ricky) and filling up on the Word of God that pulled me up and out of depression at that time.

My doctor made an appointment for me with another general practitioner, who had an interest in studying cases like mine. I don't remember much about that appointment except that it was a dead end. There was no help for me, just a whole lot of "data collecting" as far as I was concerned. I remember the look of extreme doubt on his face when I told him that I found forgiving others to be a real weight off my shoulders. He dismissed it as nonsense.

After this, my doctor decided it was time for me to see some specialists in London Ontario that might have more insight. The appointments became regular and Scott was losing several days of work each month as he accompanied me to these appointments. We decided to explore the possibility of moving to the city. The move to London would make it easier for me to keep medical appointments because I could take the bus anywhere in the city and Scott would not have to miss work.

We found a townhouse just around the corner from the school where the boys would attend. It was also five minutes by car to a great shopping mall and many other great community stores and centers. Although the townhouse needed a little sprucing up, it was a roomy and clean three-bedroom townhouse.

As we prepared to move to the townhouse, we began packing boxes and stacking them against the wall in the living room of our tiny apartment. Days of packing and sorting went by when one particular night we only had a few items left to pack. Feeling tired, I sat down on a box of linens that I had just packed and said, "I am so hungry. I could go for a cheesy pizza right now."

Within seconds of saying that, I turned my head to the patio door where I heard the sound of a vehicle coming into the driveway. We saw a big white moving van drive up to the front of our apartment. It was John and Amy. John was a carpenter and said he had a set of kitchen cupboards that he needed to pick up in London. The two of them came inside and lo and behold, in their hands they had a box of pizza. Yes! A cheesy pizza! John said that he remembered the last conversation he had with us when we said that we were moving to London. They wanted to know if we had found a place yet. He had a moving truck that was completely empty, sitting outside, and was heading to London to pick up stock from his supplier. John then asked if we would like to fill his truck with our boxes and he would drop them off at our new townhouse.

Wow! It was like God had sent John and Amy on our behalf and they didn't even know it. We had just found the townhouse and hadn't even thought of renting a moving truck to make the move and yet, God had ordained it. He had already made all the arrangements. We were just walking them out. It just goes to show that God has made a way and is thinking of the details, long before we are.

10

A Song in The Night

The first day moving into the townhouse was stressful. Reality hit me when I realized that we had moved out of my hometown and away from what I had known as "home." I suddenly became lost and could not focus. While people were moving our furniture in, I laid down and curled up on the dining room floor. I closed my eyes and just shut down to empty my head and avoid the feelings. A few moments went by, then Scott found me. He shook my shoulder.

"Are you okay?" he asked with concern on his face.

"I'm just having a hard time," I told him.

He encouraged me and brought me back to the task at hand, setting up the house and putting things in place.

The townhouse was great, but it had one drawback. The stairs that went up to the second floor butted up against the front door. As soon as you came down those stairs, you were bound to trip over or step into whatever was sitting in front of the door. It could be shoes or anything. It was worse coming down those stairs first thing in the morning and unavoidably landing with bare feet on the doormat when it was wet from the winter snow. Simply put, cold, squishy, and wet! If you were sleepy on the way down the stairs, you were wide awake by the time you hit the winter doormat!

We had only been settled into our new home for about a week and there was a lot to do. Soon the boys would be starting school. We had to get things in order quickly. We decided to go to the mall where everything that we needed would be in one place. Scott and the boys stayed in the car because it was getting a little late in the evening. I went in just to pick up a few items, thinking I'll only be a few minutes. The shopping center was bigger in the city and the multitude of aisles and abundance of choices sent me on a treasure hunt. Two hours later, I finally rolled out of the mall doors with a shopping cart piled high with stuff. I returned to the car and there was Scott, leaning on the car with his arms folded and a puzzled look on his face. It was a good thing that the boys had fallen asleep in the car. Just then, a car pulls up beside us and a young couple gets out of the car with their two little boys. I noticed they seemed to be close in age to our boys. The husband was wearing a t-shirt with the words "God's Gym" on the front of it. My husband immediately noticed and quickly approached them to get their attention.

"Hey! I noticed your T-shirt. Are you guys Christians?", he asked.

"Yes," said the husband.

"So are we!" my husband responds. "We just moved into town."

Just one shopping spree later, we had met our first friends in the city! They invited us to visit their church and we ended up attending that same church. It turns out that they also lived just around the corner from us and we would be good friends, while the boys grew up together as friends.

Shortly after we had settled into the townhouse, we discovered Tessa was pregnant again. This of course must have happened before we moved. She had a little of five kittens this time. We set up a box for her in the bottom of our closet. They all had the most beautiful markings. As they grew out of the box they loved to snuggle in one of Scott's old sweaters, that they had pulled under the bed. I would come into the room calling them, "Babies, where are you?" and they would all come jumping out from under the bed. The time came to help them find a forever home. We took them to a pet store and we watched them place them in a cage with a glass window for display. The sad eyes and puzzled look on their faces as we walked away broke my heart. I sat in the car and cried.

After Scott left for work early in the morning and the boys were off to school, my routine continued. The mornings were my devotional time, reading my Bible, as well as various Christian programming that filled the first half of my morning. I certainly continued to take a break for some laughter with Ricky and Lucy too. The re-runs never got old for me. One particular morning I was watching a program and studying along in my Bible when the message began to speak to me deeply with incredible revelation. I suddenly became excited that the answer to my healing could be ignited by the Word of God within me. I heard the preacher speak these words,

"He satisfies my mouth with good things, and renews me with the youth of an eagle." --- Psalm 103:5 (KJV)

My spirit jumped inside and the words of that scripture felt like a "prescription" to heal my entire being. It was a promise from God, to stand on and encourage my faith. He had every intention of giving me what this scripture stated. It was written right there in His Word. God cannot lie! The part that caught my attention was that my youth could be renewed like the eagle. The words were like a key unlocking a vault that was full of mysteries and answers for me. That is exactly what I needed! My youth renewed to replace painful aches, fatigue, and defeat. I needed to soar like an eagle with all the strength, vision, and freedom that I once had in my youth. God uses the eagle as an example in many scriptures. The preacher began to talk about thriving in God's presence. He shared how the eagle waits with his wings spread open, as the wind comes, he is lifted into the air. The eagle flies up above the storm clouds and is not inhibited by the storm below. He just glides upward and rests his wings, letting the wind carry him. This made things so much clearer for me. The eagle is capable of flying above the storm clouds when there is a storm. The eagle WAITS for the wind and then he lets the wind CARRY him. It was no wonder that his word says that if I wait and hope in him, I will renew my strength and mount up on wings *like* eagles.

The scripture Isaiah 40:31 speaks of "mounting up with wings as eagles".

"but those who hope (wait) in the LORD will renew their strength. They will soar on wings like eagles; they will run and not grow weary, they will walk and not be faint." --- Isaiah 40:31 (NIV)

My thought was that if I decided to thrive in God's presence, everything that was not from Him, could not exist there. He would teach me to believe in his promise, and he would renew me as the youth of an eagle. Thriving in His presence, became my goal in everything. While doing housework and every time I was not feeling well, I comforted myself with those words, "he will renew me with the youth of an eagle", speaking them out loud to encourage my faith. This was also a step that I took to stand firm in my faith because I also understood that scripture tells us;

"Faith comes by hearing and hearing by the Word of God" --- Romans 10:17 (KJV)

I was activating and standing firm in my faith based on what the Word of God says. I hear the Word of God and my faith is reinforced. It's strengthened and secured each time I would speak the Word of God. He would cause me to be victorious, renewed with strength, to soar above. Now I was looking down over my circumstances and that gave me a different point of view.

Every day I continued standing on that scripture. When I didn't feel good, when I was discouraged, when I was too tired, when I was doing the laundry, no matter what I was doing, I held on to Psalm 103:5, encouraging my faith and saying the words out loud so that my head, heart, and spirit heard it all at the same time. The ears have an active part in encouraging our body, spirit, and mind with faith and they are strengthened together as one. Perhaps this is insight about the scripture, the "spirit is willing but the flesh is weak", in Matthew 26:41. Strengthening the spirit of man is the key to overcoming the flesh. My days were different from that point on, with new direction and hope for healing.

As the years went on, I created boundaries and

separated myself from people, even Christians who caused conflict or discord. Perhaps not intentionally, but it was as though they wanted me to be the "underdog", discouraging me or tearing me down. I determined not to hold it against them. I didn't want to hold on to unforgiveness and bitterness, but I also didn't want to be influenced by their discouragement.

My friend Marilyn, once told me to guard my heart and all the things that God had for me. I met Marilyn at the airport when I accidentally encroached on her suit bag. We were both waiting for the same flight. This was when I was just fresh out of high school. My impinging on her suit bag opened up the opportunity for a little light conversation and we discovered that we were both attending the same Christian Music Conference at Estes Park in Colorado. This was my first big trip away from home. I think that for my mom it was like I was leaving for college when I took my first airplane ride to Colorado. Marilyn's words were wise and yet, I never remembered those words until much later.

"Keep your heart with all vigilance, for from it flow the springs of life." --- Proverbs 4:23 (ESV)

In my zeal, I suppose that I had poured my heart out too much without realizing that not everyone will rejoice with you to share the same vision. God had given me vision and people saw the ministry that we were doing. The clear attempts by some people to discourage us and question us should have been enough to keep me quiet and let people fall by the wayside if they were going to be so negative, but I did not see this. Perhaps I was naïve or it was because my heart really did and still does care about people no matter what. However, the revelation of the eagle's youth, along with thriving in God's presence, completely changed my response to doubters, as well as the approach to my faith and walk in Christ.

There was a dream that I received around this time as well. In the dream, I was standing on a platform at the front of a church. I was ministering to the crowd. I could hear that I was singing and then speaking. Suddenly, time seemed to stand still and the audience was frozen. A door appeared, on the wall next to the platform of the church where I was standing. It was never there before. It swung open and I knew I was meant to enter through it. Once I entered, I realized I was in some sort of courtroom. I was escorted to the witness stand. As I looked straight ahead of me, the room was kind of dark and dingy. I didn't see much around me at all, but I could see three men in business suits sitting at a long table in the distance, about 20 feet in front of me. The one in the center seemed to be the leader. Satan himself, the accuser of the Brethren. {Revelation 12:10} He began shooting questions at me like darts.

"What right do you have to stand on the platform and say these things? Who do you think you are?"

I stumbled, thinking to myself, "Why not? This is what I should be doing according to God's call on my life."

I struggled to form words that would validate myself and began to pray. Immediately to my right, a shaft of light started to brighten and I saw a group of people dressed in white who were each holding a book. I heard them sing one single note together. At that moment, I became bold. I felt "guts" and fortitude rise on the inside and I spoke up."

"I have authority to say these things because of the shed blood of Jesus that covers me and calls me his child. Greater is he that is in me and you can't stop me!"

At that moment, I stepped down from the witness stand and abruptly left the room through the door that remained open, the crowd awakened and I continued ministering on the platform that I had first left. I believe that God was affirming my calling and my right as his child through this dream. He was also reminding me that I had authority in Christ to thwart the devil's accusations. Ironically, the days ahead would reveal that I needed to be reminded of this.

One day we received an earth-shattering phone call. We were told about rumors that had spread concerning a member of the family. It was about my dad. At the time, we did not know whether or not the rumors were true. We had never heard these rumors before.

My mom and dad were divorced now. When it

happened, even as an adult, it seemed as though the weaving had come out from the bottom of my safety zone that I once knew as a child. Granted it was sometimes a rocky safety zone, but it was what I knew as a child. I fell out the bottom and there is a time of processing emotions. They say young children recover much easier because they don't understand and then they just accept the changes. I've also heard it said that when parents begin to drift apart, small children have a "sixth sense" concerning this. They become insecure, perhaps clingy, especially at night, crawling into their parent's bed, so that they can feel secure. As an adult, there was hurt, disillusionment, questions, and a time of grieving, because something had died. My parents' marriage and the image of the family unit I knew.

Now we heard of these rumors about my dad. They had seemed so "uncharacteristic" and yet perhaps anything could be true. Even after they were first mentioned, they were never discussed again. Right now, the rumor was disgustingly ugly. It hit me so hard that it took all my strength to hold back my stomach from hurling.

I thought that I had composed myself and that I had kept busy with other things to do that day, however, when the night fell, the news began to weigh heavy on me again. As I lay in bed the words just seemed to repeat, going around like circles in my mind. Feeling despair, I reached for my Bible on my bedside table and slipped on my housecoat. I then headed downstairs to the living room. Reaching the top of the stairs, I felt tears begin to fall, and then my chest tightened with pain. It was as though my heart was physically breaking. I clutched my Bible to my chest as I went down the stairs and fell on the couch, curled in a ball. I continued to hold my Bible tightly as I sat up and began to heave with tears. My chest increased with pain in the center and I could hardly breathe. I cried out!

"God I can`t bear this one. I will never be able to sing on a platform again. I`ll never be able to cope with this one. Please, Lord, you have to help me. I can`t do it."

Just then, I felt something I had never felt before. It was as though a warm thick blanket, yet lighter than air, came from behind me and fell over me, tucked me in, and then wrapped around me. It felt like the biggest, strongest arms or the most heavenly angel wings. An incredible peace came over me, the pain immediately lifted from my chest and I felt my mind suddenly become clear. I stayed still for a moment basking in this incredible peace, took a deep breath, and then opened my Bible. It randomly fell open to Psalm 63. As I read the words, I heard music flowing with the words and so I began to write a new song.

O God (Psalm 63)

O God, You are my God.
Early will I seek you in the day.
My soul, thirsts for you,
like a dry and thirsty land held at bay.

LAURIE MARKS VINCENT

I have looked for you coming into the sanctuary and I behold your power and glory

Chorus: Your lovingkindness is better than life. Your lovingkindness is better than life and as long as I live, my lips shall praise you.

O God, You are my God.
I will set my mind on you, in the night
For you are my help.
In the shadow of your wings, I take flight
Staying close to you, your right hand uphold me
and I behold your power and glory

--- (Repeat Chorus)—

Words and Music Laurie Marks Vincent

© Copyright Laurie Marks Vincent SOCAN BMI

WINGS TO VICTORY

11

Behold, Snakes & Angels

It could have been a dream, a vision, or an out-of-body experience. Whatever it was, it just seemed so real. I dreamed that I was with a group of people who were climbing a mountain. The mountain was white rock, like crystal quartz. Out of the rock grew trees and other vegetation. I did not recognize the group of people that I was with, however, I knew that we were friends. We had a common goal and kindred hearts. The day was beautiful and the sun was shining as we traveled up the mountain. It was a steady incline, but it did not seem to be a difficult climb.

We reached a point in the climb where a plateau seemed to be carved out in the side of the mountain. On the plateau, I saw people lined up at a doorway.

They were leaning against the wall of the plateau, as though they would fall off if they dare move. Somehow, I knew they were lined up waiting for something. No one entered the doorway and the line of people did not move. My eyes followed the line of people that led to a doorway. There was no hesitation as my friends and I noticed it. We walked forward with certainty and proceeded to walk through the doorway. On the other side of the doorway, we found ourselves overwhelmed with amazement. We looked around with eyes wide open. Surrounding us, it appeared to be what looked like a posh hotel lobby. A front desk with a marble countertop was located to our right. The floors were lined with rich dark marble. The ceilings were very high and they were carved out of the inside of the mountain and yet illuminated without any obvious light fixtures. One thing stood out more than anything else. In the center of the lobby was a glorious and tall water fountain that fell into a pool of water. I expected that it was just a pool of water, but as my friends and I looked closer, we discovered that the pool of water poured out into a river of water that flowed into a cave entrance and traveled through the depths of the mountain.

Just then, a young man, perhaps in his late twenties or early thirties appears in front of us. He had sun-kissed blonde hair and a handsome tanned face. He casually and warmly approached us with a smile on his face, as we notice his beach shirt, Hawaiian shorts, and flip-flops.

"Hello, and welcome! I noticed that you were looking around. Would you like to take a tour of the caverns?"

"Yes!", we said with excitement, quickly conferring in agreement, as we glanced at one another.

We climbed into a boat that seemed nothing more than a mere "fisherman's boat" with wooden slats for seats. We huddled down inside the boat while our host sat at the bow of the boat. He impressed me as the blonde beach boy, who had no inhibitions, was informal and inviting. He watched as the boat maneuvered, then we pushed off from the port located on the side of the fountain. There were no paddles, no motor to steer or propel us. We just floated along with the current of the river. In the cavern there was dimness but it was not darkness. It was lit by the incredible jewels that we saw encrusted in the cavern walls. Our eyes were captured with every jewel in the wall that we passed. My friends and I began to pull the jewels from the cavern walls and hold them in our hands to get a closer look at them. Some were beautiful rocks and when you hit them it was as though you were cracking an egg open. When the rocks were cracked open, inside, you would find a jewel. My friends collected different ones and kept them for themselves. I had looked at many of them but once I was done, I placed them back in the cavern wall.

After some time, the water suddenly became rough, as though there was a storm blowing within the caverns. We became alarmed and held on to the sides of the simple boat, which now seemed to have all the stability of a rubber dingy. I thought for sure, we were in a rubber dingy!

"The water is getting rough. Shouldn't we turn back?" I asked our tour guide with caution.

"Oh no, don't worry. It will be over soon and we'll be fine."

The little boat never crashed into the walls and remained centered. Still sitting safely now in the boat, the water settled and we continued coasting on the current of the river. We continued to admire the beautiful jewels everywhere. The light that illuminated from them seemed to bounce from one jewel to the other in subtle streams of colored light. Oh! They seemed to be "living" jewels. I continued to put them back once I had looked them over. Not one was the same. My friends, however, kept the ones that they wanted the most.

Time went on. Perhaps I had fallen asleep in the boat. The next thing I knew, I was suddenly aware that I was alone and that all my friends had left the boat. My "beach babe" tour guide was the only one in the boat besides me. We had reached another port that was a distance away from the port in the lobby.

Oh no!" I said. I was really worried, almost fearful that I had lost track of my friends. "Where did everyone go? I need to stay with my friends. Please take me back to the port that we started at."

"Don't worry," my tour guide assured me with a gentle voice.

At the very sound of his voice, I felt calm. The tone of his voice then changed as he eagerly encouraged me. "You can go to the port where you started. See, it's over there where your friends are waiting."

I protested, "But that is too far for me to swim. I won't make it."

He chuckled sweetly, "Look!"

He proceeded to get out of the boat and step into the water. I looked with surprise at what I saw.

"See!", he grins, "The water is only as high as my knees. You can walk throughout the entire cavern and the water is only this high, even in the stormy waters. I see that you forgot to keep the jewels with you that you were collecting. You can go back through the cavern and find all the jewels that you desire, then come back to meet your friends at the port over there."

"I can?", I said with wonder and relief.

"Yes! The light in the cavern will lead you back", as he points to the first port that is far off."

I laughed with joy, "Okay, I will!"

I got out of the boat and went straight to the caverns, wading through the waters. When I returned to the port where my friends were waiting, my arms were full of jewels and beautiful rocks. My friends rushed to meet me. They looked at all of my jewels as though they had never seen such a sight before. They were so happy for me, rejoicing with me and celebrating such a wonderful adventure. It's as though they knew it was a victory for me.

Our host joined in, "Well, I see you have everything that you need now."

"Yes! Thank you", I responded with a big smile.

He smiled back at me and then stepped away. My friends and I moved toward the door to leave as we said goodbye. He then waved goodbye. His face bared the look of peaceful satisfaction and joy for us, as we left through the doorway.

Leaving the hotel lobby and walking through the door, my attention was drawn again to the line of people standing there against the plateau wall. I saw a man who was first in line. He looked tired from standing and was now sitting on a small stool. It was my dad. In his hand, he held a very large jar at least 12 inches high. It was polished clean, sparkling as the sun bounced off of it. He looked at me, with a frown on his face. His eyes said to me that he was still holding on to hope, but didn't know what to do.

He shared with me in passing. "This is all I got."

The jar was empty. He then turned the jar to look inside it and then looked down at the ground as though he was ashamed.

I had concern for him but realized there was nothing I could do. This was his journey.

My friends urged me on because we couldn't stay there. We needed to continue climbing to the top of the mountain. We left with our jewels, found the path on the mountain, and continued our climb up the mountain made of white rock.

I considered this dream for months. From the very first, the message had an obvious message for me. The more I pondered the details of this dream, I gained a deeper insight and the meaning became more relevant to my life. The victory and success of what the future would hold for me depended on whether or not I used what had already been given to me, because I was in Christ. The "jewels" were there to use along the journey. They were God's promises meant for me, to stand in faith, as well as the gifts and opportunities that the Lord would bring into my life. The rocks that revealed a jewel when I cracked it open, have a very important meaning. We have a hard shell, a wall that needs to be broken down. If we surrender our will and allow God to break it down, on the inside of us, he reveals beauty that cannot be fathomed. The dream also warns me, I must not fall asleep as I did in the boat while on this journey. I must not become complacent. I then realized that the people still standing in line had already been inside. They could not move on because they failed to open their eyes or take the risk, to find the treasures inside the mountain. Some never even got " into the boat"! How could they discover what God had for them? In this dream, my dad was one who never ventured far. As I realized these and other truths, there was great anticipation and excitement in me, when I considered what the Lord might have in store.

Another dream came months later. A very wide and lush green field was before me. I walked down the center of it and reached the perimeter on the other side. As I stood there, I saw that the beauty of the lush green field had abruptly ended. Now before me was a landscape of darkness and ruin. Nothing seemed to be living or possibly thriving there. To my right there was a river like the Amazon, rushing and roaring, with great speed in the current. The dead trees bent over the dark waters and there was no life in sight ahead of me. It was my valley of the shadow of death.

Suddenly, standing in front of the dead foliage at the very edge of the river, I saw a woman. She had dark long hair, her eyes were kind and her skin was tanned dark. She was beautiful with strong shoulders. Her feminine body was muscular and fit, as though she was an Olympic swimmer. Like an Amazon woman, she was wearing a primitive cloth across her breasts and a short skirt. She was urging me to come. I knew she was an angel but I did not want to follow her. I looked behind me at the green beautiful field. There was nothing beyond the field the other way. I could not go back. It was apparent that there was no other route except to go into the dark, rough waters. I turned to look ahead and her eyes met mine again.

She called me to come, assuring me that I would be fine. I had no option but to walk forward. As I approached her, she turned and dove into the wild waters. I jumped in after her and began to swim with all my might and strength but the water's current quickly wearied me. I was feeling the struggle, swimming slower, as I continued against the current. I pulled my head above the water so that I could keep the angel in my sight but she seemed so far ahead of me. Then I noticed something else directly ahead of me. At first, I thought it was just a dead branch floating on the top of the water. Then, as I swam further ahead, it came closer. I realized that it was a snake. I panicked and screamed, struggling under the water while the snake began to close in on me, coiling himself around me. Just then, I felt a strong force pull me forward and out of trouble, taking me further down the river and up for air.

I woke up gasping, feeling very unsure of what I must face in the future. Had I journeyed through my deepest fears? What was God telling me through this dream? Was it just a dream that perhaps meant nothing at all?

I realized that whatever the case, I was rescued in the dream, and I understood that God would not fail me.

Shortly after this dream, the onset of severe headaches began to torture me for months. Although I wasn't diagnosed with Fibromyalgia yet, I also had the increasing burden, of these headaches, along with greater pain and fatigue. In addition, now Scott had two herniated discs in his back after a severe case of the flu, vomiting over the toilet. Our total income was dependent on disability cheques through his insurance. We had no money to spare at the end of the month. In faith, I was still writing songs and recording in the studio, as I was able. I thought to myself, "Right! Who was going to pay *that* studio bill?" My thoughts were concerning, but I still pressed forward.

It was during this time, that we learned that all the townhouse units in our complex were being sold off to interested buyers, by the rental company. The unit we lived in was one of the first to be chosen and sold to someone else. We had no money to pay first and last for rent somewhere else. Where would we go?

LAURIE MARKS VINCENT

12 The Snake Exposed

Our housing situation was still unresolved. Our townhouse was one of the first rental units to be purchased. We waited for the new owner's closing date on our current residence. We knew that their closing date would mean that it was our moving date. The condo corporation made empty rental units available to residents who wished to stay until they could find a new place to rent or arrange the purchase of a townhouse within the complex. A townhouse on the east side of the complex was made available to us that we could rent for the time being.

The first time that I entered the townhouse, our temporary home, I saw that the walls were painted dark purple and there seemed to be a cast of grey in the air everywhere. It was very disturbing and depressing.

We continued inspecting the condition of the townhouse. Painted on the basement floor of this townhouse, we found satanic symbols and what appeared to be a pentagram. My husband returned to the townhouse before we officially moved in and painted over the symbols on the basement floor then prayed through the house, like a spiritual house cleaning. More than any other time, I was not looking forward to this move, but I knew this was just a stepping stone.

Once the move was done and we were temporarily settled in the new townhouse, the change had distressed me. The uncertainty of where we would finally live was still hanging like a cloud over my head, weighing heavy on my mind. I can't tell you how many times, while suffering from this condition I spent days on end, doing little to nothing, laying on the couch for hours. Then I'd be okay for a few days. This was a regular occurrence.

Scott was still on short-term disability, recovering from the herniated discs in his lower back and although I never wanted to admit it, secretly I knew that my fatigue and muscular pain had increased. It was like spiraling downward in a vicious cycle, making the pain worse. I didn't want to cry anymore and I was afraid to acknowledge my fears, trying to be brave and strong. I lay on the couch day after day praying, thinking, talking to The Lord, in conversation while I was exhausted. I let my brain empty of all of my thoughts while "sleeping away the time". This seemed to be the easiest way to recover from the jolting onset of pain and fatigue.

I remember it was May of 2000 when I saw the specialist, Dr. Bell. A visit to his office determined two things.

He determined that I needed custom orthotics and he also made a clear diagnosis of Fibromyalgia, Chronic Fatigue, and a struggle with Depression. Although the diagnosis didn't come with a cure, it felt great to have a name associated officially with the pain and frustration of it all.

The headaches increased to full-blown migraines and I began visits to a pain clinic in Toronto where I received lidocaine injections mixed with cortisone, placed at the base of my head in my neck. This was because it was believed that the pain originated with muscular-skeletal problems due to the old neck injury that could have ricocheted to my jaw and skull. This was the injury that I suffered when Scott and I were first married.

In the summer, one of my visits to the Toronto pain clinic began with great alarm. The pain was so intense by the time that we reached the clinic that the physician monitoring me immediately sent me to the hospital emergency, requesting an MRI for fear of an aneurism.

The hospital emergency was informed of my arrival by the pain clinic. They were kind and thoughtful and had reserved an empty waiting room for me, with the lights turned low. This helped to ease the pain from my headache. While waiting quietly there in the vacant waiting room, closed to the general public, Scott made a phone call to our friend Sanj that we had worked with at 100 Huntley Street. We had always stayed in touch with Sanj. His laughter and his influence were infectious in our walk with God. He even shared a story about us, at our wedding reception. He was now a pastor and living in Toronto at the time. To my surprise, about 20 minutes later, Sanj finds us in the waiting room where we were waiting to see a doctor.

"How did you know we were here?" I asked him.

"Scott called me. Remember?" he replied.

It was good to see him and we talked for some time and then he said to me, "Laurie, have you ever had any involvement in witchcraft?"

Other questions came one by one. Each one seemed to lead to a dead end. I had no solid answers to his questions. Pastor Sanj knew that God had given him a revelation. I needed to be set free from the enemy's hold and he was determined to be thorough and follow the Holy Spirit's leading.

"Doesn't matter," he said. "Laurie, we're going to pray. I'm going to lead you in a prayer to denounce all these things. Even though I had never intentionally been involved or subjected myself to anything that was not of God, we took precautions. In a moment of weakness, sometimes we let our guard down through fear and despair and the enemy has a way of getting hold of us and making trouble. Even if you've never had anything to do with these things, just follow through and repeat after me as we pray together."

That was it! I had let fear and despair open doors by ignoring them instead of taking authority over them. This allowed the enemy to fester his plan, I thought to myself.

I followed through as Pastor Sanj prayed and we renounced any activity such as witchcraft, in the name of Jesus. Just then, as we finished praying, I felt a sensation as though a snake had slid down and away from my right leg. The pounding headache and migraine sensations left immediately, although my body felt as though it had been through the wringer. I have never had any migraine and occipital pain again with such intensity. Could this have to do with the dream that I had of the snake in the dark waters, while the dark-haired angel accompanied me? I had been waging a war and didn't realize that I became oppressed under it instead of being victorious over it.

This is not the first time that there was an encounter like this. Once again, I'm recalling the time when we were living in Tillsonburg. It was late in the evening while Scott was working late. The boys were tucked in bed asleep and I was working on the details of an event that I would be ministering at.

My memory took me back to a night when I had identified the fight in the spirit. Remember when I called Nancy in Tulsa? Yes, I really "heard" a victorious sound, that was not of this world. As I was sitting at the dining room table, working through my papers, I looked up. There was something evil glaring at me through the dining room window. Responding more in fear, than the authority in Christ that I should have had, I ran to the phone to call Nancy. When I told her what I saw, we began to pray. Now, you may think I was hallucinating but that's not so. After a few minutes of praying on the phone, the Lord allowed me to hear what was happening in the spirit realm.

While she prayed, I know without a shadow of a doubt that I heard the voices of angels singing. All the notes harmonized like a chord on the piano. The angels sang three solid notes blended, which must have lasted for at least 2 minutes.

I think to myself, "I could be a looney case", but I know what I heard and it was not of *this* world.

The truth is, this was a call to victory and warfare over the powers and principalities in the air. Just like the angels, when we sing, our praise reaches heaven and exerts victory over the enemy.

WINGS TO VICTORY

13 New Wings

While living in this temporary home, we were fighting harder. I needed to walk in my healing by thriving in God's presence, trusting in Him, and hiding in Him even more. Some of the new songs had been completed and I had a few of the soundtracks to get started. We would start to explore what God had in store next.

We took another leap of faith. We asked the Lord that if it was his will, he would enable us to buy one of the townhouses in the complex. We still had no money for the first and last month's rent and so we couldn't rent anywhere else. We also had no down payment available either. This was probably the craziest move yet. It was scary, exciting, and full of uncertainty for us. We had no idea how we could be approved for a mortgage on

Scott's short-term disability income.

As we discussed the possibility with the realtor and the bank, it was determined that we needed a co-signer to purchase the townhouse that we had our eye on. Weeks went by, and God had not put anyone on our minds to ask. No one had even crossed our paths that we felt we should ask.

In the middle of it all, I happened to be having a "good day". On that day, we were out running errands and ran into our old friend, Brenda. She was so excited to see us and immediately she wanted to have a visit and catch up. We met later at a coffee shop and exchanged life stories. She was not well and had just recently received a large settlement from a car accident. Perplexed by our current housing situation, she offered to co-sign for us using the settlement money as equity for our mortgage. Her offer overcame us with tremendous emotion. We were humbled, overwhelmed, relieved, and elated!

After putting our offer in motion, it was approved and the papers were signed in the Lawyers office in October. That was a great birthday present for me. We moved into a newly renovated townhouse on December 23, 2000. It was a mild but snowy night. God had proven himself, time and time again. This is the time when we celebrate Christ's birth, the greatest gift of all, and yet, he was still giving us gifts. His blessing was felt beyond measure. This was a move that I truly looked forward to. I was excited to set everything up in our new home.

I had made up my mind that if I was called to serve in this capacity, through music ministry, then God would have to continue sustaining me and grant me healing. At this time, I was led to open a business called "Ministry Networks". I set up my home office, serving other Christian Music artists through various services such as radio servicing (airplay on Christian radio) graphic design, and web design.

While I couldn't operate in full-time ministry, in some way I felt this would support those who were in music ministry also. Ministry Networks was the first company to foster this kind of service to Canadian Christian Music Artists who desired airplay on Christian Radio in Canada. Christian Radio was a newly established and growing vision in Canada that was becoming a reality.

Time had progressed and I had managed to produce more soundtracks of the songs that I had written for another CD. They were slated to be a part of a CD in the future. It was about 2001/2002 when I found myself very quickly rising to appear on television programs such as "Spirit Alive", "100 Huntley Street" with Rev. David Mainse, and "Celebrate" in New York, along with the Miracle Channel and "Life and Faith" on The New PL in London Ontario (Now CTV London). Yet I still was not free from the pain I faced, flipping back and forth with good and bad days. I had to make sure I rested well before these television appearances.

On a particular appearance at 100 Huntley Street, I was

singing a song called, "He Leads Us On. Later, a woman reached out to me and told me that she was sitting about 8 feet from her TV kneeling on the floor as she listened to the song I was singing. There were a pair of nail clippers sitting on the top of her TV set. At one point in the song, the nail clippers flew at her and missed her. She said it was as though someone had swiped their hand and pushed the nail clippers with force across the room. She explained that she had received some insight. She noticed that after her son had been to a birthday party where the children played a game of Dungeons and Dragons, she realized that there had been some troubling things happening with her son and in their home. Realizing that there was a demonic entity in her home, she took authority over it and it was gone.

The words to this song no doubt were an irritation to this demonic entity.

He Leads Us On

There's a rushing wind,
and if you listen, you can hear it,
Move across this land, in the ones
who bare the name of God's son.
Into the darkness splitting the night,
with the power of his Light

We will stand of army thousands
We're called to freedom,
by the stripes and the scars

of the Mighty Warrior.
We're armored and chosen
to stand in this fight,
with the Mighty Warrior. He leads us on.

With our armor on,
and praise in our song, we will be strong.
Our spirit will see if our hearts will believe
his promises meet every need.
He hears every word, reaching on high
as we answer the battle cry.

Other Kingdoms are shattered
when we stand together.
Take hold the victory, won at the cross.

We will stand of army thousand.
We're called to freedom,
by the stripes and the scars
of the Mighty Warrior.
We're armored and chosen
to stand in this fight,
with the Mighty Warrior. He leads us on

Words and Music Laurie Marks Vincent –

On the Cd "Love So Amazing"

© Copyright Laurie Marks Vincent SOCAN BMI

It was my second invitation to appear on another show known as Spirit Alive. Scott was not able to accompany me on this trip and so I took the train there. In the studio, I filmed my music segments on the last day. I then returned to the host home where I was staying for the night. In the middle of the night, I awakened with so much neck and shoulder pain that I could barely hold back from yelling out loud. I got up out of bed, took the cordless phone, and went to the safest place I knew; the bathroom.

The bathroom seemed like a place where I wouldn't disturb anyone. I called Scott, crying on the phone. In excruciating pain, I was having anxiety and I just wanted to go home. He tenderly comforted me and said that he would pray for me. He talked, I cried, he talked, I cried. We were five hours apart from each other and so going home was not an immediate option. After I hung up the phone, I heard a knock on the bathroom door.

"Hello?" "Are you okay?"

I opened the bathroom door astonished, yet embarrassed. It turns out that there was a pastor and his wife who lived in the basement apartment. I had no idea! They had heard everything that I said through the vent on the bathroom floor! The Pastor and his wife led me into the living room. It was Pastor Barry Maracle and his wife Tammy. They sat with me and listened to me with compassion, as I shared that I was dealing with Fibromyalgia. It just so happened that Pastor Barry and Tammy had been holding "healing services". They had seen many women healed of Fibromyalgia during their services. How God-accidental is that? They counseled me and listened to me with great care and then they prayed with me. I simply accepted whatever God led them to pray. I felt secure and as though I was completely covered. There was no indication that God's power had touched me or that His hand had come down like a "bolt of lightning" and healed me. They finished praying and I found myself calm, filled with peace, and ready to go back to sleep. I thanked them and returned to my room.

The next day I returned home on the train. As I thought about my time there, I thanked God for the opportunity to serve and also for the love and prayer that I had received. Scott and the boys were there to meet me when the train came into the station. We never discussed the phone call that we had the other night since the boys were with us and I seemed to be fine.

Daily, I continued to hold on with hope for healing. I continued dwelling on the scripture and kept the words on my lips.

"He satisfies your desires with good things so that your youth is renewed like the eagle."

-- Psalm 103:5 (NIV)

Several days had gone by, and then two weeks, when I realized one morning that I had been waking up EVERY morning, without pain. My sleep was refreshed and I felt as though my heart had been "unstuck" and "lifted". You see, one of the things about Fibromyalgia is that your days are inconsistent. It took me several days in a row before I had even realized that God had healed me.

I asked the Lord, speaking out loud, "Did you heal me?" I felt stupefied! Astonished!

IN THAT VERY MOMENT, I KNEW that God had healed me. I had this inner assurance inside of me that came with such joy. I stepped into a leap and danced around the room laughing with joy. Laughter and joy filled the room even though it was just me alone. I felt like the caterpillar who went through a transformation and now, like a butterfly, I was able to fly. There was no lightning bolt, just his simple love, and gentleness that had removed what had bound me.

LAURIE MARKS VINCENT

14

Mysteries Revealed

I continued to write, record, and minister where I was called, whether it be a church or women's event. I also now did speaking engagements because now I had a testimony of God's amazing faithfulness and healing to encourage others in the faith too. Sometimes, it was simply just to sing for an event and that was wonderful too Over the years, I have seen the Lord minister to many women in special ways through my story and the songs. He has never failed to be present and meet each one where they were at that time.

Many years later on a Saturday afternoon, I sat alone in the living room. As I was surfing the channels on the television, I stopped at this television program that I would have normally just passed by. The reason that I stopped was that I had heard just a few words of something that seemed familiar to me. A young woman began to explain how this old ghost woman would approach her and wake her in the middle of the night. My mind went back to the dream when I awoke and found the old woman's head hovering over me. The young woman continued to explain that the old ghost woman would come and harass her, waking her night after night. Sometimes she couldn't breathe and so she paced the floors almost all night. She had insomnia and constant muscular pain. She was describing Fibromyalgia! She was describing the effects that I faced as I struggled to breathe that night I had the dream. Then, the young woman described what the old ghost woman looked like to a police artist. When the sketch was done, it was shown on the TV screen. I gasped with surprise as my eyes fixed on the image when it came on the screen. The sketch of the ghost woman was the same face that I saw hovering over me on the night I had that dream.

Professionals have labeled this ghostly phenomenon. It is known as the "old hag syndrome" and is said to happen due to stress, fear and anxiety when a person is traumatized. I did indeed face fear, stress, and anxiety. There were clear signs of it as I became numb and suppressed my emotions. Avoiding them meant I didn't have to deal with the process. However, it's too coincidental that the ghostly hag looks the same to more than one person. The mind simply can't see the same thing that someone else sees if it's supposed to be just a "mental" image. The old ghostly hag woman truly is a dark ugly menacing spirit. Her purpose is to wear your defenses down, even to the point of death. She possesses fear, anxiety, stress and wants to impose them, breaking down and bringing weakness to those she attacks. I'm not saying that I wasn't experiencing trauma, but I do believe that the enemy was using this to his benefit.

This part of my journey and this quest was now much clearer.

The scriptural riddle that I had once pondered, had a greater depth and meaning for me.

"Now faith is the substance of things hoped for, the evidence of things not seen." -- Hebrew 11:1 (KJV)

Jesus uses the mustard seed as an illustration so that we can understand how faith increases in our lives.

In Matthew 17:20, Jesus said, *"Because you have so little faith. Truly I tell you, if you have faith like a grain of a mustard seed, you can say to this mountain, 'Move from here to there,' and it will move. Nothing will be impossible for you."*

Therefore, to understand how faith works, we must understand the mustard seed. It is just a tiny seed, no larger than a spec. However, when a mustard seed spreads naturally from one plant, growing wild, it can cover a whole hillside. It spreads as the wind carries the seed, spreading it across the land. The mustard plant can be a tree. It is also a well-rooted, strong, and stalky plant that stands upright with shoots like branches that lift upward. The trees can grow up to 20 feet tall *and* 20 feet wide. It can grow in dry climates and thrive even in clay or sandy soil. It can grow in hot, dry weather or cool, wet climates too. It's clear why Jesus used the mustard seed to compare with faith. Our faith can be tested in the "dry times" when we feel like there is a drought in our spirit. Our life feels like a desert, during the most difficult of circumstances. Yet, even in the dry times, he is causing our faith to be challenged and to grow as we draw closer to him in difficult times.

The mustard seed will also not graft with another plant either. You will never be able to create a "half mustard seed and half carrot seed" for example. The mustard seed will always produce one kind of plant. The very same mustard plant that it always has produced. Just like faith, it must be 100% faith, no doubt. You can't mix a little faith with your doubt. You must be convinced that it is by faith and faith alone. It is also interesting to know that if you cut down to the trunk of a mustard tree, it will grow back again. So even when we are pruned and our faith is shaken, seemingly cut off, we can overcome. We can come back stronger than ever. This is a great illustration of how our faith rejuvenates. The next question is, what causes our faith to rejuvenate. Like the mustard seed, it grows and matures as it is watered. We all have a measure of faith, perhaps even as small as the mustard seed. It's the nurturing of that seed that causes it to grow and strengthen.

"Faith comes by hearing, and hearing by the Word of God." -- Romans 10:17

Any good word that confirms and lines up with the Word of God will encourage our faith. Also, the Word of God instilled and continually planted and nourished in us will reap faith. This is exactly what happened when I kept holding the words of Psalm 103:5 near to me, using them to encourage me and strengthen me daily. Eventually, I reaped what the Word of God promised.

I was renewed with the youth of an eagle, just as that scripture describes in Psalm 103:5

Now, concerning Hebrews 11:1 that always felt like a riddle to me?

"Now faith is the substance of things hoped for, the evidence of things not seen". -- Hebrews 11:1

Life had become clearer between the physical and spiritual, the seen and unseen, and the hope of what was yet to come, that God had planned for me.

Three things stand out in my mind God used to keep me focused, bringing me to victory in this area of my life.

1) Learning to trust in God and sometimes re-learning.

2) His song in my heart, with joy and gratitude

3) His Word on my lips, making faith evident and a reality.

It was now easy to see that nothing was impossible with God. (Luke 1:27) A more modern translation, the International Standard Version, of Hebrews 11:1 says,

"Now faith is the assurance that what we hope for will come about and the certainty that what we cannot see exists.

It means that just because we can't see something with our eyes, that doesn't mean it isn't there. When it finally comes into reality, that is when it is the proof, or evidence, of what we have been believing for because we wait and trust in God. Sometimes, I was my own roadblock. The key was to understand that his Word increased my faith, to receive from him and get past this roadblock. It did require taking "me" apart and putting me back together so that I would be whole again. It was more of him and less of me. God really did have a purpose in this whole journey.

The blue butterfly became a favorite of mine afterward. I became curious, discovering the name of this butterfly. It's known as the "Blue Morpho" and has some very specific special qualities that speak to me about my journey. It is native to the Amazon rain forest. Do you remember the woman in my dream who stood at a river like the Amazon? This is a revelation for me. I must go through the difficult waters for my own transformation. The Blue Morpho butterfly is also attracted to light. Always reaching for the light, it often rests in places where there is light. When the butterfly is resting, the wings are closed, like two hands placed together, sitting on its back. When the wings are closed you can see the underside of the wings, which are not blue. They are a dull brown or grey, with intricate patterns and circles that look like several eyes on the underside of the wings. This is to deter enemy predators. The interesting part about this is that when their wings are open and flying, this is the only time you see the brilliant blue color on their wings. It gets even more fascinating. The color isn't really blue. It's an iridescent effect that happens when the light hits its wings. It's caused by the diamond formation of the minuscule scales on the surface of their wings. This speaks to me so loud and clear about not just my journey but everyone's journey. He refines us, like coal under pressure, that eventually becomes a diamond. It's not until we open our spirit, open our heart, like the butterfly opens its wings, to let the light in. When spread our wings and fly, just like the iridescent effect on the butterfly's wings, this is when we shine. It's when we fly and the light of his love reflects on us. This happens when we open our wings and try to fly. Let me say it again; this happens when we open our hearts, nurture our faith and chase after God, the Light in our life. We fly! It's no wonder Psalm 103 was speaking clearly about renewing the youth of the eagle. It's about waiting on God and flying in faith.

Later, an examination by my family doctor proved that although I had suffered from Fibromyalgia and Chronic Fatigue for 13 years in total, I was now free from any of the symptoms of that condition. Hope had been placed where Depression once lived. Roots that grew deeper, nurtured my faith that changed my world. I could fly!

This wasn't the only miracle! In 2003, our youngest son Kyle had received miraculous healing. He had a severe lazy eye and his prescription for eyeglasses required prism lenses. The television was on, and the show was a healing service where Pastor Benny Hinn was talking to a lady who had been sitting in a wheelchair. Our little boy took a leap of faith when he her get out of her wheelchair.

He said out loud, "If God can do that for her, then he can heal my eyes too."

We responded with an absolute, "Yes!"

At the end of the program, it was announced that Pastor Benny Hinn would be in Toronto at the Air Canada Center for a healing crusade. Immediately Kyle spoke up.

"Can we go?"

We agreed that we would plan to go. He held his faith firm, never wavering. We told him that the gas for the car would cost us more than we usually budget and so the lunch we pack in the cooler would help us save money. In the weeks that followed, something on the car suddenly needed repair. It was minor but necessary, especially if we were going to Toronto for the healing crusade next week. Kyle was present, staying silent while he overheard this conversation, but he didn't get nervous. As a little boy, he saw us not having enough and this had affected him. Yet, he did not waver. He knew that the money we set aside for our trip had to be used to fix the car.

Later that day I told my husband we were out of milk but there wasn't enough money to spare until his paycheck. The money we spent on the car repair took the extra $50 in our bank account. I suggested to Scott that he go to the Heavenly Hamper, a food bank run by a church in the city.

"Explain that we don't need groceries, but ask if they have any powdered milk just to get us through the next week."

Scott agreed and Kyle asked if he could go with dad. The two of them left and returned quite a bit later with an astounding story.

They arrived at Heavenly Hamper and my husband explained, asking if they had any powdered milk. The dear lady at the food bank happily responded.

"Yes! We do. Let me get some for you."

She left the front reception and went through the doors

to where the groceries were. Scott said that they waited for quite some time.

"We wondered how long it would take for her to find the powdered milk?"

He continued to tell me the story.

"Finally! She came out and there was this strange look on her face."

"What do you mean?" I asked him.

"She handed me a bag of powdered milk and then she said she was sorry that it took so long because the Holy Spirit spoke to her."

Perplexed and amazed, I asked, "Really?"

"Yes," he responded. "She handed me a $50 bill and told me that the Holy Spirit told her to give this to us. Her exact words were -- because you're going to need it."

Imagine how much Kyle's faith was strengthened when he realized God had replaced our gas money to get to the healing crusade.

The day came, leaving early in the morning for the very first service of the healing crusade that weekend. We made our way to the upper balcony seats to the right of the stage. Kyle was sitting between us. The service began with beautiful worship. I looked over at Kyle and he had his arms lifted high in the air, but his hands were flopped over and hanging down. I was so blessed by his child-like faith. It just looked like total surrender. It was a proud moment for mama.

Kyle also had a condition called "Hyperhidrosis". This is the excessive sweating of the hands and feet. No doubt he was always bothered by sweat because he hated that his glasses would slide down his nose when he was sweaty. Right now, his focus was for Jesus to heal his eyes.

Pastor Benny Hinn could not be seen on the stage while the worship was happening. We continued in the Lord's presence as we sang the songs. I'm not sure if Kyle ever sang a note, but with his hands lifted high, his focus was Jesus.

Just then, Pastor Benny Hinn came out on the stage. The music quieted as he stood up. He stepped forward on the stage with exuberance. He lifted his arm and with his finger, pointed to where we were seated.

"Jesus is walking by and healing someone right over there."

A brief second or two passed as Kyle opened his eyes. He was having trouble seeing. He tapped Scott's arm.

"Dad, dad, I can't see."

Scott told him to take off his glasses and rub his eyes.

Maybe his eyes were tired because he was up really early. When Kyle removed his glasses his eyes suddenly grew big with a look of surprise on his face. He could see without his glasses!

We took him down to the front of the stage. A kind elderly gentleman was standing there who was wearing a white doctor's coat. He was asking everyone in the line, what God had done for them. When we reached him, Kyle explained what happened and showed him his glasses. This elderly gentleman happened to be a doctor. He took Kyle's glasses in his hand and examined the lenses. Then, he turned them to see their thickness against the glare of the light.

"This looks like a pretty strong prescription. Tell ya what. Can you read something far away for me?"

"Sure!" Kyle responded. "What do you want me to read?"

The gentleman looked around, then quickly pointed to an advertising banner that was hanging on the wall behind the stage and off to one side. Kyle read the large words in the center of the banner and continued reading.

"Whoa! Wait a minute! What are reading now?" the doctor asked.

Kyle was quick to respond, "The little words at the bottom of the banner sir."

The doctor's face beamed as he chuckled. "Son, Jesus has healed your eyes! Praise the Lord!"

Kyle had received his healing. This was only the first service and Pastor Benny Hinn didn't have to say a word or preach or sermon or touch him. It was simply Jesus responding to Kyle's faith amidst the praise and worship that day.

We returned home that day and the following Monday I called an optometrist and made an appointment for Kyle. In the meantime, Kyle returned to school. There was quite a response from his friends and teachers when Kyle explained why he did not need to wear his glasses anymore. What a witness that this was to all of his grade 8 classmates!

Two weeks later, the optometrist verified that Kyle's eyesight was restored to 20-20 vision.

"This is not a condition that corrects itself so quickly. He has not been wearing these glasses for very long. How did you say this happened?"

We told him the story, explaining that we had been to a healing service and Jesus healed him.

"Well, whatever you did, it certainly worked!" he remarked.

Kyle and I both shared our miracle story, as I made another appearance on 100 Huntley Street TV show. It was great to be back at 100 Huntley Street and the Crossroads family, which was part of our Canadian legacy and Christian heritage. It was also in their new building since they had relocated from the heart of Toronto to Bampton Ontario by this time.

My CD "Love So Amazing" was released in 2004. It included carefully chosen songs, that I wrote during the time I suffered for 13 years. I cannot forget the generous donation that made this entire CD possible. It was truly a step of faith when I wrote down my heart and shared it with someone that God has prompted with interest. The CD has gained momentum since, seeing many hearts touched by this healing testimony, as well as the ministry through the songs.

I would so love to go back into the studio and refresh these songs with new production and vocals one day. Especially, certain songs that are specifically about this journey.

The eternal message of God's Love and His son Jesus Christ can be found because he ministers through music. He meets those in need, in the same way, that I was in need, during that time.

WINGS TO VICTORY

15

The Whole Woman

I'd like to add just a few thoughts that came to my memory afterward. While living in the little white house, I later recalled a conviction about eating "quick fix" meals. Boxed meals, especially because of preservatives, where you "just add water", were removed from family meals and more natural foods and vegetables were added. Not always, but as much as possible, our meals consisted of food that was as unprocessed and came naturally from God's hand. Shopping around at the right farmer's market has made this even more possible. Meat without hormones along with fruits and vegetables came at nearly half the price and right out of the local farmer's garden.

During the 13 years of illness, my addiction to starchy

carbohydrates and sugar was a strong instigator. It was likely one of the reasons for all of the highs and lows in my moods and energy. Although I have received supernatural healing, God wants me to know what my body needs and what affects my health. Today I have learned that diet does contribute to inflammation in the joints and muscles. Although it has been a challenge, a low glycemic index diet is a big help. However, I will NEVER give up chocolate. Even if I fall off the "bandwagon", I have a foundation of standards to fall back on. It just helps to keep my "addiction" to starches and sugars under my thumb and my health on track. This is just sensible for anyone, no matter how healthy you are.

I remember just a few weeks after the Lord had healed me that I had experienced some of the same symptoms again. The pain and all the symptoms of Fibromyalgia began to manifest again.

I asked the Lord, "Did I sin? Was I wrong? Lord, didn't you heal me? What did I do?"

I was a little frantic as all the familiar pain flooded my body. I heard the Lord speak to my heart sternly, but with comfort.

"Oh yes! I healed you, but now I want you to learn to maintain what I've given you."

At that moment, if I was hearing him speak to me so clearly, I didn't want to stop asking questions.

"Then Lord, please tell me what I need to do."

Then I suddenly had an understanding that I had never had before. I understood that God was asking me to reinforce my health.

He directed me to take a multi-vitamin in the morning and a Vitamin B Complex at lunch. Within a few short weeks, I was back on top of my health and I could go the whole day without needing to take a nap.

What was He showing me? A little research helped me to understand that perhaps when several things in my life collided at once, this affected my nervous system. I was newly married, recovering from an injury while becoming pregnant. then living for a short time under the roof of my parent's broken marriage, then a new mother, two Caesareans, and complicated postpartum depression. No wonder I felt trapped emotionally, socially, psychologically, and physically worn. All of this had tasked my nervous system and I was broken down. It took a 13-year journey to take it apart with God's help, start from scratch, go to the root and allow him to give me the missing pieces.

The simple fact is, that our bodies are on loan from God. Our bodies are an earthly dress for our eternal soul and spirit. He has asked us to maintain and care for what He has given us. We are accountable for the care of our bodies and how we treat ourselves, spiritually, emotionally, mentally, AND physically. I can have bad habits, but I have to ask myself, "Do I love myself?"

Most importantly, I have to ask myself, "Who do I love more? Me or God?" Since he will always love us more than we love ourselves, He requires that we are good stewards of all the things he has given us, including our bodies.

"Do you not know that your bodies are temples of the Holy Spirit, who is in you, whom you have received from God? You are not your own; (20) You were bought with a price, therefore honor God with your bodies."

-- 1 Corinthians 6:19,20 (NIV)

The 13 years with Fibromyalgia have been a deciphering between spiritual encounters, physical bombardment, and the struggle for emotional and mental wholeness.

We receive our salvation in faith. We ask in faith and receive his grace (favor that we don't deserve) because we believe. If we do not believe, then we do not receive. It's that simple. That moment we believe, then his grace is available to us. We simply ask and God forgives us of our sin. I'll say it again. We simply believe when we ask him and we receive. However, what is sometimes forgotten is that the journey has many winding roads, twists, and turns that bring us *to* that very moment when we finally realize that we need him. It's then a reality that we are born with inherited sin. It is the human condition, and we need the Saviour to cleanse us. When we realize that our need is deep, it takes us to the next place in our relationship with him. It is the same with our healing. We receive our salvation "by faith" and so it is with our healing as well. Those words "by faith" are powerful.

"By faith" simply means that we take him at his word and trust him fully to do as he has promised.

The most convincing revelation for me is the fact that THE God of the universe lives in me! His Holy Spirit and all that he is dwells within me.

"My old self has been crucified with Christ. It is no longer I who live, but Christ lives in me. So I live in this earthly body by trusting in the Son of God, who loved me and gave himself for me." – Galatians 2:20 NLT

I realize that his indescribable power makes him more than capable to meet my every need. I have to pinch myself because this is such an awesome truth. If such is the case, I wonder why I don't walk with more power in my life, to be the overcomer that He has called me to be? Unquestionably, I am drawing from his grace. It is also certain that the faith I am drawing from is not my own, but it is the power of God, his faith, dwelling in me. Yes God has faith, or he couldn't make it available to us. We are all broken, even at our best, but his faith and his strength are PERFECT. He is never weak or small, nor is he double-minded. The power of God's faith does not even have room for doubt as small as a grain of sand. It is 100% concentrated faith and it's available to me. His faith, working in me, is more than enough to believe and receive.

There's a story in the book of Mark about a father who is desperate for his boy to be free from a demon.

Jesus asks the Father, "How long has this been happening?" [Mark 9 NLT]

He replied, "Since he was a little boy. 22 The spirit often throws him into the fire or into water, trying to kill him. Have mercy on us and help us, if you can."

"What do you mean, " If I can?" Jesus asked. "Anything is possible if a person believes."

The father instantly cried out, "I do believe, but help me overcome my unbelief!"

Now, I must take you back to the part of this story that shows you where faith stops and doubt starts.

The father says to Jesus, "....*Have mercy on us and help us **if you can**.*"

I can picture Jesus deeply focused with compassion, looking into the man's eyes. Jesus must have raised one eyebrow as he asked him, *"What do you mean, " If I can?" Jesus told him, "Anything is possible if a person believes."*

The moment that a question is posed about Jesus' availability or ability to grant a need, doubt has entered, hope can turn to doubt and a measure of your faith is watered down by mixing it with doubt. Jesus had to question the father so that he would consider his unbelief. What I find so enlightening now is the Father's response.

*The father instantly cried out, "I do believe, but **help me overcome my unbelief!**"*

The Father admitted his need for help so that he would overcome his doubt. This is total SURRENDER. After this, Jesus rebuked the demon and set the young boy free.

What happens next is quite astounding. The boy lay there, appearing as though he was dead. A murmur could be heard through the crowd, "He's dead." Jesus took the boy by the hand and the boy lifted his head and sat up.

Just like the murmur in the crowd, even when the answer you receive is not what you're looking for, don't believe the murmur of doubts and negative reports around you. Negative words cancel out the effectiveness of your faith. Your words either reinforce your faith or reinforce your doubt.

Jesus said, *"I tell you the truth, you can say to this mountain, 'May you be lifted up and thrown into the sea,' and it will happen. But you must really believe it will happen and have no doubt in your heart."*

--- Mark 11:23

Jesus did not say that we should ask **him** to speak to our mountain of circumstances. He says that *we* have the authority to speak to the mountain, and we will see change if we believe and do not doubt. We must speak it out. We must make our declaration of faith out loud. Contrary to the negative murmur that could be heard from the crowd, the boy appeared to be dead, but he was not dead. You cannot trust what you perceive in the natural realm when regarding your personal miracle. If you do, doubt will stir in your heart. Stand firm in your faith, holding to Jesus' hand and he will cause you to rise to your feet.

We wonder if God always heals. I believe because the work was already finished on the cross, yes. Since Christ has borne our infirmities on the cross, it is not subject to who he chooses should or should not be healed. He bore them for every man and woman and child when he took our sin to the cross.

"Surely He took on our infirmities (pain and suffering) and carried our sorrows; yet we considered Him stricken by God, struck down and afflicted." – Isaiah 53:4 (Berean Study Bible)

"That it might be fulfilled which was spoken by Isaiah the prophet, saying: " He Himself took our infirmities And bore OUR sicknesses."

– Matthew 8:17

It's worth repeating. This is about the journey until his

Word accomplishes that which he has ordained for your life. The finished work of the cross, completed in you.

"Being confident of this very thing, that he which hath begun a good work in you will perform it until the day of Jesus Christ:" – Philippians 1:6

It is the lessons in the journey that bring wisdom, maturity, and insight. You may need to read parts of this book over again until it truly embeds in your spirit. Our journey brings us to the place where we can finally receive healing and victory over the circumstances. When you are struggling, do not pray that God removes your doubt. Pray that he help you with your unbelief. Pray that he prepare your heart to receive. Sometimes we are not ready to receive and it requires a deeper revelation of our fears and unbelief. Then, we must be willing to surrender.

Yet, never doubt. Remain in your declaration of faith, and keep speaking to your mountain. This is exactly what I was doing when I used Psalm 103:5 to encourage my faith. I was speaking to my mountain and claiming God's promise. Through every part of our journey, and turn in the road, we see more of him, for who he is and how he sees us... through Eyes of grace.

*For it is by grace you have been saved, through faith--and this is not from yourselves, it is the **gift** of God--*

Ephesians 2:8 (NIV)

LAURIE MARKS VINCENT

ABOUT THE AUTHOR

Laurie Marks Vincent is a Christian inspirational speaker, songwriter, recording artist, visual artist, and author. Yes, all of those things make her a very artsy and creative gal. Her passion is to touch people's lives with the talents that God has given her and to use them promptly. There is a season, a time, and a place for everything.

Since the age of 16, she has traveled to minister at churches. First singing special music, and then after being married, children's ministry with her husband Scott, as well as a speaker and music ministry. Today,

Laurie shares her music and story of God's healing in her life, at women's events, conferences concerts, and churches.

Her devotionals air weekly on Christian Radio, the WJIC Network, Racman Christian Radio, and the Cpop Network.

Through the years, she has been voted "Best Female Vocalist" twice at regional talent searches. She has also received several recognitions including a nomination in the top ten, for a Heritage Award for the best music video "My Deliverer" by the Artists Music Guild, Nashville, Tennessee. The same video received a top ten nomination at the Lamplight Film Fest.

Laurie and her husband Scott, reside in London Ontario. Brandon and Kyle are now grown and living nearby with their beautiful families. Brandon and Raylene have three children, and Kyle and Sandra have two children. Laurie and Scott are "Nana and Papa" to five grandchildren as of 2022. We're all looking forward to what God has in store for the future.

Currently, she is the host of a TV program that begins airing in mid-2022, called Grace Talk on Best Life TV Network. The program features inspiring and courageous testimonies of faith from people around the world. Her music and books along with other media projects and her inspiring messages of faith will continue to be shared on bestlifetv.org

Laurie along with her husband Scott continues to minister. Their ministry together is a department of ACT International, a licensed charity organization that aids to mobilize Christians to do the will of God in the arts. Her passion is to complete another very important recording project that includes a very crucial song and evangelism video production called "The Passion Project".

You can support "The Passion Project" and Laurie's ministry by giving an offering at the link below.

More about her ministry, music, media, and booking

http://www.LMVministry.com

"For now we see through a glass, darkly; but then face to face: now I know in part; but then shall I know even as also I am fully known."

1 Corinthians 13:12 (KJV)

Made in the USA
Coppell, TX
31 March 2022